THE MOST BEAUTIFUL NAMES OF ALLAH

SAMIRA FAYYAD KHAWALDEH

Goodword
B·O·O·K·S
www.goodwordbooks.com

First published 2001
© Goodword Books 2003
Reprinted 2003

Goodword Books Pvt. Ltd.
1, Nizamuddin West Market
New Delhi 110 013
e-mail: info@goodwordbooks.com
Printed in India

---

www.goodwordbooks.com

THE MOST BEAUTIFUL NAMES OF
ALLAH

*I love you My Beautiful One
Yours Forever
Love
April 2008*

Introduction

Our century will be remembered for its marvellous achievements in many spheres. We should be proud of ourselves. We have made the world a healthier place—more pleasing to the eye, more comfortable, and more interesting. Yet, with all the wars our times have witnessed, and the deadly arsenals which have been built up, the brain-children of devilish minds for devilish purposes, we must admit that, somewhere, a big mistake has been made; or a significant fact has been forgotten by almost everyone.

The most sinister thing about us twentieth-century people is that we are conditioned to feel that the world is a better place, and that we are happier human beings than our ancestors ever were throughout history. But, to put it simply and bluntly, we are not. On objective scrutiny, we shall certainly become aware of the increase in mental and psychological disorder around us; most of which owes its existence to the absence of a reasonable and convincing answer to the biggest question of all times: WHY?

Man, from early childhood, needs to be assured that the affairs of the world are not chaotic; that everything runs according to a perfect and accurate scheme. Even an autumn leaf withers and falls at a time and in a way which have been carefully pre-set. If our education is based on this conception of universal wisdom and order, future generations will be less disturbed by any nastiness or unpleasantness that may confront them.

Fear in our world is the same as in the jungle. Now, man is afraid of man; of disease, of death, of nuclear war, of poverty, of betrayal, of starvation and so on. It is true, man can never be rid of fear; but fear can be made less damaging if mingled with hope. Fear of death is offset by the hope of an eternal happy life to which one can actually look forward. Fear of disease becomes much less if one knows he will be loved and generously rewarded for his endurance; and like the athlete who exerts himself, he will actually enjoy the efforts he makes if he is confident, or has hopes of winning.

So, the present attitudes must be altered for our own benefit. There is a complete blueprint,—a philosophy of life and an interpretation of existence presented to mankind by Allah. We have only to embrace it in order to obtain mental, spiritual and even physical well-being. The story of mankind is summed up in the following Qur'anic Verses: Expelling Adam and Eve out of Paradise, Said He, 'Get you down, both of you together, out of it, each of you an enemy to each; but if there comes to you from Me guidance, then whoever follows My guidance shall not go astray, neither shall he be miserable; but whoever turns away from My remembrance shall have a life of extreme hardship' (20:123-124).

What is there that can be worse than the loss of a sense of direction? Modern man is short-sighted, he sees his next step, but not the road ahead nor the destination it leads to. Practical and busy as he is, with a mind "scientifically" oriented and moulded, all he knows is the answers to his immediate problems. Faced with any problem beyond that, he stands helpless.

Hard-heartedness is another symptom of the malaise of the age. Man's soul is far withdrawn that the word of truth cannot reach it. You see people fettered by compulsion to satisfy their own selfish needs; goodness cannot penetrate their hearts. It can neither enter nor issue forth.

Their hearts were hardened, and Satan made their deeds seem fair to them (6:43).

Love is turned into a form of body-worship: mutual care and good feelings are out of fashion; suicides, battered babies, neglected parents, are all sacrifices, not to the heathen gods as in ancient days (at least that was unselfish), but to our egos.

Have you considered the man who has taken his own caprice to be his god? (25:43).

Such are the hearts described here: Then your hearts became hardened like stones or even harder: for there are rocks from which rivers come gushing, and others split, so that water issues from them, and others crash down for fear of Allah (2:74).

Surely, there is always hope. A blow might split the rock and release the sleeping spirit!

Spiritual deprivation will never allow man to experience peace of mind. He will try to cover up the hunger of his soul with pompousness, pretensions, the accumulation of wealth and, quite often, aggression. What can a mind sans peace give to the world? Only social upheaval and disquiet. Of course, people can never be transformed into angels, but they can be turned in the direction of being more 'human' if we preserve their essential characteristics: the moral, the spiritual and the emotional.

The only way to do this is to renew man's relationship with the one God, Allah; and to open a channel that links the creature to his Creator. Man should recognize Him in love, trust and even in wholesome fear. Many things and images have mistakenly been named 'gods.' But, there is, and there can be, only one True God, with one Will. Otherwise, contradiction and not harmony would have prevailed in the universe.

Allah demands worship from us, in word, in deed and in thought. The last form is called *dhikr* (remembrance) and is the backbone of the faith.

Surely in the creation of the heavens and earth and in the alternation of night and day there are signs for men possessed of minds; who remember Allah, standing, sitting and lying down, and who reflect upon the creation of the heavens and the earth. (3:190-191)

Remembrance of Allah permeates man's life with the quality he needs most: peace and repose. It shows him things in their right perspective: man is to be positive and active, but at the same time, detached.

No part of the matter is yours. (3:128)
and
All is in the hands of Allah. (3:154)

Trusting Allah like this, transforms one's life: Surely in the remembrance of Allah all hearts are comforted. Blessed are those who have faith and do good works; blissful is their end. (13:28-30)

This is the core of the Message sent to mankind by Allah through a mortal, Muhammad, who did his best to convey it to all people. It is the right of every man to receive the Message, and the duty of every Muslim to proclaim it. However, it is not as simple as that; Islam, Muhammad's Message, is a way of life that cannot be transmitted by word only. First, it must be practised, then preached.

Muslims, for centuries, have abandoned the true spirit of Islam, — a great tragedy, not just for them, but for humanity in general. Even those who proclaim it, have, in many cases, failed to understand the nature of the Message. Nowadays, due to the intensity of ideological conflict in the world, they have transformed Islam into another ideological theory.

Some of them go even further in that direction and forget that it is a Faith, descended from a Divine Source, and that before we explain the Islamic economic and political systems we have to establish the faith and strengthen man's relationship to Allah. Did not the Prophet Muhammad, peace be upon him, preach the faith in Makkah for thirteen years? There, in Makkah he built a religion, demolished falsehood, and stirred in the hearts of men the love for Allah. It was only when the faith had been firmly rooted in Madinah that the rules and details of the Islamic social order started to be revealed.

People may interpret this historical fact in different ways; but, one thing we may be sure of: the sequence of events cannot be reversed. In other words, we should never try to persuade people to construct their society upon the Islamic model, unless it is solely on the basis of belief in Allah, the one God. The structure of the Islamic Law (*Shari'a*) by itself, i.e., in contrast to the Creed (*Aqida*), will certainly on application be superior to any other, man-made system.

But it falls short of the grandeur and beauty it might obtain if based on and cemented with the spirit of the faith.

Hence, expressions like, 'Islam says,' 'Islam wants,' 'Islam insists' and 'Islam orders,' are, in a sense, misleading and they reflect the unhealthy state of affairs at present. What is Islam? It is submission to Allah and the following of His injunctions. It is a mental and emotional state, not an entity that dictates and certainly not one that can be substituted for Allah. In the Holy Qur'n, the term Islam never occurs in such contexts as commence with 'Islam says', etc. It is always Allah who desires and orders, and who loves and hates. This is more direct. And the Faith, as presented in the Qur'an, is not another cold and flat ideology, but an active and warm relationship between man and Allah.

Allah, in the Islamic concept, is the One Being who created and who supports everything and to whom we are accountable. The first principle to take in consideration when talking about Him is in the Qur'anic verse: "Like Him there is naught; He is All-hearing, All-seeing" (42:11). Here it is stated clearly and unequivocally that we can never have an image of Him. But, at the same time, it is stated that He hears and sees; so, He has qualities, some of which can be described and named—to contemplate when we remember Him. Those are merely the ones mentioned in the Qur'an[1], attributed by Allah to Himself, and in the *hadith* of His Messenger. Anything beyond that is unauthorized and should be disregarded.

However, there are verses in the Qur'an that describe Him in words which usually have a physical significance, such as, "then He sat Himself upon the Throne," (7:54); "to be formed in My Sight," (20:39); and "Allah's Hand is over their hands." (48:10)

It is thought by some that these words are metaphorical, symbols of authority, vigilance and power [2]. This is the nature of language they say, and of Arabic in particular. But the best thing to do is to follow the tradition of the Messenger and his Companions who completely abstained from asking about, or discussing, such matters. 'Sitting' (*istiwa'*) is known to us, but when attributed to Allah it cannot give the same meaning; it becomes a matter of the Unseen

---

[1] For the English interpretation of the Qur'anic texts we have referred to two sources: *The Koran Interpreted*, by Arthur J. Arberry (London : Oxford University Press, 1964), and *The Holy Qur'an. Text, Translation* and *Commentary*, by A Yusuf Ali (Brentwood, Maryland : Amman Crop., 1983).

[2] See, for example: A. Yusuf Ali, *The Holy Qur'an. Text, Translation and Commentary* (Brentwood, Maryland: Amman Crop. 1983), p.355. See also Abu Hamid al-Ghazali, *'Ihya' Ulum al-Din*, Vol. I (Cairo: Mustafa Babi al-halabi, 1939), p. 113.

in which we have to believe without first-hand knowledge; and asking about it is an 'innovation' that leads astray.[1] This applies to all such expressions as mentioned above. Thus, the second principle is to avoid thinking about or trying to find explanations for those words when attributed to Allah.

To try to understand Allah is beyond our ken. We can understand the human mind, examine nature, but we can know Allah only through His creation.

Instead of knowing Him in terms of images and shapes, we know Him in terms of names, attributes. They are called the Most Beautiful because they attribute to Him qualities of goodness, perfection and truth, even name like the Avenger and the Afflictor refer respectively to his just punishment and His power and wisdom.

Allah has the Most Beautiful Names; so call Him by them, and keep away from those who blaspheme His Names—they shall

---

[1] The Prophet, peace be upon him, said, "Verily he among you who lives [long] will see great controversy, so you must keep to my *sunna* [tradition] and to the sunna of the rightly-guided Rashidite Caliphs—cling to them stubbornly. Beware of newly invented matters, for every invented matter is an innovation and every innovation is a going astray and every going astray is in Hellfire." (*Abu Da'ud* and *Trimidhi*).

assuredly be punished for their misdeeds (7:180).

To blaspheme His Names means to give them the same meanings as the have when applied to men. For example, 'the King,' 'the Just' and the 'Witness' are Divine Names and at the same time applicable to men. But they have different meanings in each case. Allah is not King in the way that a human being would be.

We are told by the Prophet, peace be upon him, that "Allah has ninety-nine Names, a hundred minus one. Anyone who learns them goes to Paradise." (*Bukhari, Muslim*). The ninety-nine Names are listed in another *hadith* related by *Tirmidhi*.

"Allah" is the only proper Name among the Ninety-Nine. The rest are attributive. When a man once called out in his prayer, "O the All-merciful One, O the All-compassionate One!" one of the unbelievers heard him and said, "Does Muhammad not claim that he worships One Lord? Why then does this man call upon two gods? In answer to such questions, the following verse was revealed:

Call upon Allah, or call upon the All-merciful; whichever you call upon, to Him belong the Most Beautiful Names (17:110).

Names of glorification, such as the Glorious, the Lord of the Kingdom, the Omnipotent, the All-powerful, etc., make up about a third of the Beautiful Names. They indicate His power, and majesty, and are comprehensive; that is, each covers a number of meanings, all befitting Him. There are also twenty-two Names signifying benevolence and kindness, such as the All-merciful, the Oft-returning, the All-loving, the All-provider, etc. Some Names, such as the Maker, the Originator, indicate His creative energy. Others, like the Reckoner, the Just, suggest besides His power over His creation, our accountability to Him.

Allah loves to be glorified and praised by His Names when invoked.

Allah has the Most Beautiful Names; So call Him by them. (7:180)

Calling Him by His different Names puts emphasis on what one needs most on particular occasions; for instance, if one needs guidance, he should call upon Allah, the Guide; if deliverance, upon the All-deliverer; if mercy, upon the All-merciful, and so forth. However, calling Him by His proper Name suffices for all attributes.

Remembering His Names blesses one's life; it has many benefits: At bedtime, the Prophet, peace be upon him, used to say, "Allahumma, in Your Name I live, and in Your name I die" (*Bukhari, Muslim*).

He also said, Any servant who repeats thrice every morning and every evening: "In the Name of Allah; with whose Name nothing on earth or in heaven can be harmful; He is the All-hearing, the Omniscient!" will not be harmed by anything (*Abu Dawud*).

If anyone afflicted by anguish or sadness, says: "Allahumma! I am Your servant, son of Your servants. My forelock is in Your Hand. What You have decreed for me is carried out. Fair is Your Judgment upon me. I ask You by every Name that is Yours, by which You have named Yours, or which You have revealed in Your Book, or which You have taught to any of Your creatures, or which You have kept with You in the knowledge of the Unseen—to make the Glorious Qur'an the spring of my heart, the light in my breast, the lifting of my sadness and the end of my anguish," Allah will wipe out his sadness and sorrow and replace them with joy (*Ahmad*).

There is the Name, 'the Most Glorious' (*al-Ism al-Azam*). It is the Name by which if He is called, He answers. However, Muhammad, peace be upon him, did not specify it to avoid its misuse.

Aisha, the Prophet's wife, said to him, "O Messenger of Allah! Teach me the Name of Allah by which if He is called, He answers." He told her to perform ablution, say her prayer, then call upon Him while he was listening. When she sat down to do so, the Prophet said, "Allahumma! Guide her!" Then she said, "Allahumma! I ask You by all Your Most Beautiful Names; what we know of and what we do not. And I ask You by Your Glorious Name, the Most Glorious, the Great, the Greatest, by which if You are called, Your answer, and if asked, You give," The Prophet said, "You have attained it, you have attained it" (*Ibn Majah*).

This Name is believed to be a combination of several Names.

Finally, this work has been undertaken with the aim of rekindling the light of His knowledge, and the revival of His remembrance in people's hearts. We also hope to introduce to English-speaking people the genuine concept of the True God, through His Divine Attributes. Working on the subject was greatly rewarding, and we hope that reading it will be rewarding too.

Amman,　　　　　　　　　　　　　　　　　Samira Fayyad Khawaldeh
Jordan.

 Allah

"Truly, I am Allah; there is no god but I; therefore serve Me" (20:14). Allah is the most sacred Name that indicates the Being Most High, His oneness and His godly attributes. "Say: 'He is Allah, One; Allah, the Everlasting Refuge, who has not begotten, and has not been begotten, and to whom there is no equal'" (112:1-4). No god is to be worshipped other than Allah. "And call not upon another god with Allah; there is no god but He. All things perish, except Himself" (28:88).

Things exist by the will of Allah. "When We decree a thing, We need only say: 'Be', and it is" (16:40). He supervises their affairs: "Surely your Lord is Allah, who created the heavens and the earth in six days, then ascended His Throne, ordaining all things," (10:3),........ and to Him they shall all return," "And He is God; there is no god but He. His is the praise in this world and in the hereafter; His too is the power supreme, and to Him you shall be recalled" (28:70).

While other Names are attributes, 'Allah' is the proper name of God, that has never been given to any other being in Islam or *Jahiliyya* (pre-islamic times).

No god is to be worshipped other than Allah. "And call not upon another god with Allah; there is no god but He. All things perish, except Himself." (28:88)

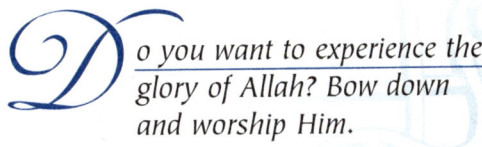

Do you want to experience the glory of Allah? Bow down and worship Him.

The Compassionate

AR-RAHMAN

"Say: 'He is the All-merciful'" (67:29).

Rahman is a special intensive form derived from *rahma* (mercy). In human beings, *rahma* means 'tenderness of the heart'. Yet, when attributed to Allah it means 'granting blessings and warding off evil, through grace, condescension and beneficence.'

For this reason, *Rahman*, like the Name Allah, is not applied to any but God.

Allah's mercy in this world is general: given to the believer and the unbeliever. He provides for them and gives them health and what they ask for. "We bestow Our mercy on whoever We will, and shall never deny the righteous their reward" (12:56). "Allah created one hundred mercies, then He put one of them among His creatures by which they love one another, and Allah has the other ninety-nine" (*Al-Bukhari*).

We must always ask for

Allah's mercy and grace, and call Him by this name; our deeds by themselves, do not qualify us to go to Paradise.

Also, we ought to begin any important action after saying these words, "In the Name of Allah, the All-merciful, the All-compassionate" (1:1).

Believers are merciful to all creatures. A man was forgiven all his sins when he drew water out of a well in his shoe and gave it to a very thirsty dog.

"Our Lord, we believe; therefore, forgive us, and have mercy on us, for you are the best of the merciful."
(23:109)

Have compassion for all Allah's creatures.

AL-RAHIM

The Merciful

"There is no god but He, the All-Merciful, the All-compassionate." (2:163)

Rahim is another attribute, also in the intensive form derived from *rahma* (mercy). Here 'mercy' implies pity, patience and forgiveness, all of which sinners need. "O My servants who have transgressed against their souls; do not despair of Allah's mercy; surely He is the All-forgiving, the All-compassionate." (39:53)

Allah is more merciful than vengeful. In a Holy Hadith, He says, "My mercy surpasses my wrath." (*Al-Bukhari, Muslim*)

In the Hereafter, Allah is All-compassionate to the believers only.

"My mercy embraces all things, and I shall prescribe it for those who are god-fearing" (7:156). "Do you think this mother would throw her infant child in the fire? Allah is more merciful to His servants than she is to her child." (*Al-Bukhari, Muslim*)

To be merciful is essential for a Muslim: "The merciful ones will be given mercy by the All-merciful. Be merciful to those who are on this earth, and the One in heaven will have mercy on you." (*Al-Bukhari*)

"My mercy embraces all things, and I shall prescribe it for those who are god-fearing."
(7:156)

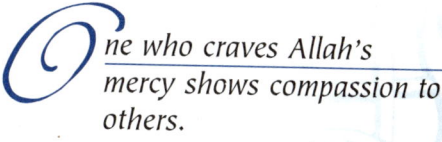

One who craves Allah's mercy shows compassion to others.

The Sovereign

AL-MALIK

"He is Allah, there is no god but He. He is the King." (59:23)

Allah owns the universe and controls it. "Blessed be He in whose hand is the Kingdom; He has power over everything" (67:1). "To whom belongs the Kingdom of the heavens and the earth; and He has not begotten a son, and He has no associate in His sovereignty" (25:2).

Allah is the Lord of all sovereignty. "Say: 'O Allah, Master of the Kingdom, You bestow sovereignty on whom You will, and take it away from whom You will.'" (3:26)

True meaning of Kingship is an attribute only of Allah. "Then exalted be Allah, the True King. There is no god but He, the Lord of the noble Throne." (23:116)

It is solely by the will of Allah that men are given Kingship. "Allah gives Kingship to whom He will." (2:247)

Allah is in need of nothing and of nobody. Yet, everybody

and everything are in need of Him. "Say:'I take refuge with the Lord of men, the King of men, the God of men.'" (114:1-3)

To Him belong Kingship, majesty, power and wealth. "So glory be to Him, who has control of all things, and to whom you shall all be recalled." (36:83)

"Say:'I take refuge with the Lord of men, the King of men, the God of men.'"
(114:1-3)

The law of Allah is applicable to everyone.

The Holy
AL-QUDDUS الْقُدُّوسُ

The All-Holy: "He is the King, the All-holy." (59:23)

Allah is free from imperfection, shortcomings or need, and He is the One to whom are attributed all good and beautiful Names. "The son of Adam calls Me a liar, and he has no right to. He reviles me, and he has no right to. He calls Me a liar when he claims that I cannot recreate him, and he reviles Me when he says I have a son. I am exalted and I take no spouse and no son." (*Al-Bukhari*)

The origin of the word *quddus* is *quds* which means 'purity' and 'integrity.' Yet people confuse the attributes of God and associate other things or beings with Him, hence the need for revelation. "They underrate the might of Allah. But on the Day of Resurrection, He will hold the entire earth in His grasp and the heavens shall be rolled up in His right hand. Glory be to

Him! Be He exalted above any that they associate with Him! (39:67). 'Hand' here, as attributed to Allah, is not the physical hand we know. We must not try to explain or imagine what it really is. Allah is independent of our time, space and matter. "Like Him there is naught" (41:2). "His is the loftiest likeness in the heavens and on the earth." (30:27)

The angels call Allah by this name all the time: "We proclaim our praise and call Your Holy" (2:30). And the Prophet, peace be upon him, used to say in his prayer: "Praise and Holiness be to Your, Lord of the angels and souls." (*Muslim*)

"We proclaim our praise and call Your Holy."
(2:30)

Actions carried out in absolute sincerity and solely for His sake are acceptable to Allah.

The All-peace

AL-SALAM

"He is the King, the All-holy, the All-peaceable." (59:23)

True peace comes in this life to those who recognize and serve Allah. "Say:'Praise belongs to Allah, and peace be on His servants whom he has chosen.'" (27:59)

And in the next life, "their greeting, on the day when they shall meet Him, will be 'Peace!'" (33:44)

In times of fear, anxiety and hardship, a believer finds peace with Allah. "Say:'I seek refuge with the Lord of the Daybreak from the evil of what He has created.'" (113:1-2)

A believer, by following the will of Allah, lives in peace with himself, with other human beings, with the universe and with His Lord, "There has come to you from Allah a light and a Book Manifest whereby Allah guides to the paths of peace whoever follows His good pleasure, and brings them forth from the darkness into light." (5:15-16)

Believers spread peace amongst themselves and in the world. Muhammad, peace be upon him, said, "By the One in whose Hand is my soul! You do not enter Paradise until you believe, and you do not believe until you love each other. Shall I tell you of something to do so that you may love each other? Spread peace amongst yourselves." (*Muslim*)

"*Allahumma*! You are the All-peaceable and peace is from You; Blessed be You, O possessor of Majesty and Nobility!" (*Muslim*)

"Say: 'I seek refuge with the Lord of the Daybreak from the evil of what He has created."'
(113:1-2)

Make Peace at any price.

The Giver of Peace
AL-MU'MIN

"He is the King, the All-holy, the All-peaceable, the Giver of Peace." (59:23)

Allah is the real giver of security. Only by being faithful to Him can one feel truly secure and have no fear at all. "Which of the two parties has a better title to security? Tell me if you know the truth. Those who believe, and have not confounded their belief with evil-doing-shall surely earn salvation." (6:81-82)

Security here means the peace one feels in his heart issuing from faith. Besides, Allah promised His loyal servants that their faith would be firmly established, so that they would live in peace and security instead of suffering and persecution. "Allah has promised those of you who believe and do righteous deeds that He will surely make them successors in the land, just as He made their ancestors successors, and that

He will surely establish their religion for them that He has approved for them, and will give them in exchange, after their fear, security." (24:55)

Allah never fails the faith others place in him; and His promise is genuine and never broken: "This is what Allah and His Messenger promised us, and Allah and His Messenger have spoken truly." (33:22)

Thus, in this world of uncertainty and spiritual loss, there are people who lead their lives untouched by its misery and distress: "Surely those who say, 'Our Lord is Allah' and then go straight, shall have nothing to fear or to regret." (46:13)

>
> "This is what Allah and His Messenger promised us, and Allah and His Messenger have spoken truly."
> (33:22)

The simplest way to keep away from other's evils is to keep others away from one's own evils.

The Protector
AL-MUHAYMIN

"He is the King, the All-holy, the All-peaceable, the All-faithful, the All-preserver." (59:23)

Allah is the great preserver and is watchful over everything. "There is no creature that crawls, but He takes it by the forelock." (11:56)

Allah controls creation and guards it from corruption and loss, except as He will. The Qur'an has similar attributes.

"And We have sent down to you the Book with the truth, confirming the Book that was before it, and guarding it." (5:48)

This means that the Qur'an is the criterion by which we judge the other revealed Books.

He is witness to what his creatures say and do. Nothing escapes His knowledge, not even the secrets in people's hearts. "And whoever has done an atom's weight of good shall see it, and whoever has done an atom's weight of evil shall see it" (99:7-8). "He reigns supreme over His servants. He sends recorders to watch over you." (6:61)

O God, I seek Your protection from misery and grief, from weakness and laziness, and from the burden of loans and from things that will make others overcome me. (*Al-Bukhari, Muslim*)

"And We have sent down to you the Book with the truth, confirming the Book that was before it, and guarding it."
(5:48)

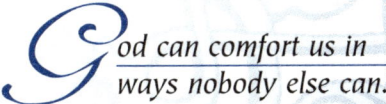

God can comfort us in ways nobody else can.

The Almighty

الْعَزِيزُ
AL-AZIZ

"Thy Lord is the All-powerful, the Almighty." (11:66)

Allah is the Conqueror that is never conquered and never harmed, because of His might, glory, force and pride. "All that is in the heavens and the earth magnifies Him; He is the All-mighty, the All-wise." (59:24) "Glory be to your Lord, the Lord of Glory, above all imputations: And peace be upon the apostles; and praise be to Allah, the Lord of the Universe." (37:180-182)

The faithful worshipper knows that glory is obtained only in servitude to Allah. "Those who take unbelievers for their friends instead of believers—do they seek glory in them? But glory altogether belongs to Allah" (4:139). "They say, 'If we return to the City, the mightier ones of it will expel the more abased,' Yet glory belongs to Allah, and to His Messenger and to the believers, but the hypocrites do not know it." (63:8)

Invoking Allah by His Most Beautiful Names is an act of worship. A bedouin once said to the Prophet, peace be upon him, "Teach me something to say." The Prophet replied, "Say, 'There is no god but Allah, the One with no partner. Allah is the Greatest by far; much praise be to Him. The Lord of the Worlds be praised; and there is no power and no strength save in Allah the Almighty, the All-wise.'" The bedouin said, "This is for my Lord. What is for me?" The Prophet, peace be upon him, said "Say, 'O Allah! Forgive me, have mercy upon me, guide me, and provide for me." (*Muslim*)

"They say, 'If we return to the City, the mightier ones of it will expel the more abased,' Yet glory belongs to Allah, and to His Messenger and to the believers, but the hypocrites do not know it."
(63:8)

Bow at the very name of God.

The Irresistible
AL-JABBAR

"He is the King, the All-holy, the All-peaceable, the All-faithful, the All-preserver, the Almighty, the All-compeller." (59:23)

Allah is the one who oblige His creatures to do whatever He wishes. Man's will is granted by Allah, so he can act only with His permission.

"But you cannot will, except as Allah wills." (76:30)

Allah's will is imposed on all and no will is imposed upon Him. "He shall not be questioned as to what He does, but they shall be questioned." (21:23)

It is reprehensible to give the name of *Jabbar* to human beings. *Jabbar* applied to a man means a 'tyrant;' but a tyrant is always brought down by Allah. "So Allah sets a seal on every heart which is proud and arrogant" (40:35). "Frustration was the lot of every powerful, obstinate transgressor. In front of such a one is Hell." (14:15-16)

Jabbar also means the One who sets right the affairs of His creatures: He is the Lord of the Universe "Who created me, and Himself guides me, and Himself gives me food and drink, and whenever I am sick, heals me, who causes me to die, then brings me back to life." (26:78-81)

"Frustration was the lot of every powerful, obstinate transgressor. In front of such a one is Hell."
(14:15-16)

Whoever loves to meet Allah, Allah loves to meet him.

AL-MUTAKABBIR

The Superb

"He is the King, the All-holy, the All-peaceable, the All-faithful, the All-preserver, the Almighty, the All-compeller, the All-sublime." (59:23)

Allah has all pride and glory. He is beyond need and is without imperfection. He is beyond the qualities of what He has created. "Glory be His in the heavens and on the earth." (45:37)

Pride, an exclusively godly attribute, must never be claimed by human beings. Allah hates proud people who elevate themselves above others. "Allah does not love any man who is proud and boastful" (57:23). "Pride and glory are My garments, whoever claims them, I torture him." (*Muslim*)

Punishment for pride in this life is spiritual blindness: "I shall turn away from My signs the arrogant and the unjust; so that even if they see every sign, they will not believe in it." (7:146).

And in the Hereafter they will be thrown into Hell. "Shall I tell you about the people of Hell? Every harsh, niggardly and proud man." (*Al-Bukhari, Muslim*)

The Prophet, peace by upon him, said, "He who has in his heart the weight of an ant of pride will not enter paradise." A man then asked, "What if one likes to dress well?" The Prophet, peace be upon him, replied, "Truly Allah is beautiful and He loves beauty. Pride is to deny the truth and despise people." (*Muslim*)

Yet to His good servants Allah is kind and loving: "Whoever comes to me walking, I come to him running." (Al-Bukhari).

Lodge God in one's heart: that is the best of states.

The Creator
AL-KHALIQ

"Say, 'Allah is the Creator of everything, and He is the One, the Omnipotent'" (13:16). Allah created things out of nothing with no precedence and for a purpose known only to Him. "Allah is the Creator of everything; He is Guardian over everything; to him belong the keys of the heavens and the earth." (39:62-63)

What can false gods create? "This is Allah's creation; now show me what those have created who are apart from Him!" (31:11)

They have no power, even in front of a fly. "Surely those upon whom you call, apart from Allah, shall never create a fly, though they banded together to do it, and if a fly should rob them of anything, they would never retrieve it from him. Feeble indeed in like measure are the seeker and the sought!" (22:73)

We should observe the wonders of creation around us

in order to feel the greatness of Allah. "Surely in the creation of the heavens and earth and in the alternation of night and day there are signs for men possessed of minds who remember Allah, standing and sitting and on their sides, and reflect upon the creation of the heavens and the earth, saying 'Our Lord, You have not created this in vain. Glory be to You!'" (3:190-191)

Allah also has another name, *Al-khallaq* (the All-creator), the intensive form of *Khaliq*.

"Is not He, who created the heavens and earth, able to create the like of them? Yes indeed; He is the All-creator, the All-knowing."
(36:81)

The entire world created so favourably for man is a blessing of Allah.

AL-BARI'

The Maker

"He is Allah, the Creator, The Maker." (59:24)

Allah created matter, then He made out of its elements different sorts of things and beings. *Bara'a* (the root of *bari*) implies a process of evolving from previously created matter. "And He originated the creation of man out of clay, then He fashioned his progeny from a drop of humble fluid, and He shaped him, and breathed His spirit into him." (32:78)

The general qualities of things and beings made by Allah are in the right proportions. "Surely We have created everything in right measure." (54:49)

The balance in creation is a wonderful phenomenon. It is the most obvious sign that leads to Him. "You do not see in the creation of the All-merciful any imperfection. Turn up your eyes: do you see any fissure? Then look once more, and yet again:

your eyes in the end will be dazzled, and weary." (67:3-4)

'Fear God, for He is the one Who sets right all that concerns you. Read the Qur'an and keep remembering God. For then you will be remembered in the heavens. And that will be a light for you on the earth.' (*Ahmad Ibn Hanbal*)

> "And He originated the creation of man out of clay, then He fashioned his progeny from a drop of humble fluid, and He shaped him, and breathed His spirit into him." (32:78)

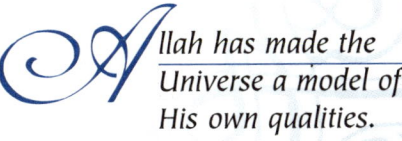

Allah has made the Universe a model of His own qualities.

The Shaper

AL-MUSAWWIR

"He is Allah, the Creator, the Maker, the Shaper." (59:24)

Allah shaped His creatures and made them numerous and varied. He gave each a form which was unique and distinctive. "We created you, then We shaped you" (7:11). "It is He who forms you in the womb as He will." (3:6)

Allah made everything in the best form; adapted to the ends for which it was created. "And He shaped you, and shaped you well, and provided you with good things." (40:64)

In addition to the beauty and grandeur of all Allah's creation, He has endowed man with special aptitudes, faculties and capacities, and a special excellence which raise him at his best to the position of Allah's vicegerent on earth. "We indeed created man in a most noble image." (95:4)

Only a self-deceiving man

ignores all that. "O man! what deceived you as to your Lord who created you and shaped you and wrought you in symmetry and composed you after what form He would?" (82:6-8)

>
>
> *"O man! what deceived you as to your Lord who created you and shaped you and wrought you in symmetry and composed you after what form He would?"*
> *(82:6-8)*

The world is stricken by evil so that man can learn to be good.

AL-GHAFFAR

The Forgiving

"Lord of the heavens and earth, and of all that lies between them, the Almighty, the All-forgiving." (38:66)

Allah forgives the sins, small and big, of His worshippers. "Yet I am All-forgiving to him who repents and believes, and does good works, and at last is guided." (20:82)

Allah can punish people and display their shameful doings; but because of their good deeds He does not betray them. Muhammad, peace be upon him, said, "Allah, praise be to Him, brings His servant close and hides him and asks him: 'Do you know such and such sins?' The servant says, 'Yes, my Lord.' And He asks him again until he admits all his sins. Allah then says, 'I have concealed them in your life and today I forgive them.' And he is given the book of his good deeds." (*Al-Bukhari, Muslim*)

"O son of Adam! As long as

you call me and plead with me, I forgive you all that you have done, and I do not mind. O son of Adam! If your sins reach the clouds in the sky and then you seek My forgiveness, I forgive you and I do not mind. O son of Adam! If you meet Me with the earth as a container full of your sins, and then you meet Me associating none with Me, I will come to you with its fill of forgiveness." (*Tirmidhi*)

Allah is also named *Al-Ghafur,* and *Al-Gafir,* "Forgiver of sins." (40:3). *Ghafur* is more forgiving than *Ghafir,* and *Ghaffar* is the most forgiving.

"Yet I am All-forgiving to him who repents and believes, and does good works, and at last is guided."
(20:82)

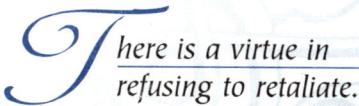

There is a virtue in refusing to retaliate.

AL-QAHHAR

The Dominant

"Glory be to Him: He is Allah, the One, the Omnipotent." (39:4)

The universe runs according to laws laid down by Allah. No one can reverse them and those who try to break them suffer. This involuntary submission to the laws made by Allah is one meaning of Islam. "And to Him has surrendered whoever is in heavens and on the earth, willingly or unwillingly, and to Him they shall all be returned." (3:83)

Allah has absolute will and the absolute power to implement it. His will is free; nothing can hinder it. "And if He visits you with affliction, none can remove it but He; and if He visits you with good, know that He has power over all things." (6:17)

People may worship gods other than Allah, but what sort of power do such gods have? "Say which is better, many gods at variance, or Allah the One, the Omnipotent." (12:39)

When one tends to disobey Allah, one must think of His infinite power and that He may punish the sinners in any way He will. "Had Allah willed, He would have taken away their hearing and their sight. Truly, Allah is powerful over everything." (2:20)

Only He, may He be exalted, may force natural phenomena to behave in an unusual manner. The Prophets' miracles are examples of this: "We said, 'O fire, be cool to Ibrahim and keep him safe.'" (21:69)

Al-Qahhar is the intensive of *Al-Qahir* (the Compeller) which is another Name of Allah.

"Had Allah willed, He would have taken away their hearing and their sight. Truly, Allah is powerful over everything."
(2:20)

The most worthwhile work is the preaching of Allah's word.

AL-WAHHAB

The All-giving

"You are the munificent Giver." (3:8)

Allah gives abundant blessings perpetually. He gives all who are in need what they need, for no purpose other than giving and for nothing in return. He gives, in this life, to the deserving and the undeserving, to the good and the evil. "Say: 'Surely bounty is in the hand of Allah; He gives it to whoever He will.'" (3:73)

There is no counting of Allah's gifts; yet few people appreciate them "And [He] gave you everything you asked Him for. If you reckoned up Allah's blessings, you could never count them; surely, man is sinful and thankless!" (14:34)

Allah is the only One you may petition and the only One to expect good from. "Those you serve, apart from Allah, have no power to provide for you. So seek your provision with Allah, and serve Him, and be thankful to Him." (29:17)

Prophethood and Revelation are the most precious of Allah's gifts to mankind. "Today I have perfected your religion for you, and I have completed My blessing upon you, and I have approved of Islam for your religion." (5:3)

Wahhab is an intensive form of *Wahib* (Giver).

"And [He] gave you everything you asked Him for. If you reckoned up Allah's blessings, you could never count them; surely, man is sinful and thankless!"
(14:34)

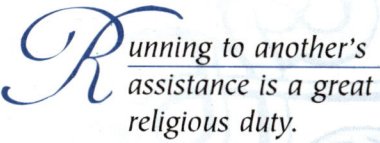

Running to another's assistance is a great religious duty.

AL-RAZZAQ

The All-provider

"Surely Allah is the All-provider." (51:58)

Allah provides sustenance for His creatures. He, alone, is the giver of their livelihood. "Is there any creator, apart from Allah, who provides for you out of heaven and earth? There is no god but He." (35:3)

Allah provides nourishment and cover for the body, and for the soul, knowledge and guidance. "This is Our provision, of which there is no end." (38:54)

Allah created all beings and He never forgets them. Birds, animals and the lowest orders are provided for, too. "How many are the creatures that cannot find for themselves, but Allah provides for them and you! (29:60)

Razzaq is an intensive form of *Raziq* (Provider), "But surely Allah is the best of providers." (22:58)

This is the Name to call when one is in need. Besides,

as Allah provides for us, we must give to others freely. "Expend of what We have provided you with before death comes upon you and you say, 'O my Lord, if only You would reprieve for a while, so that I may give in charity and be among the righteous.'" (63:10)

"How many are the creatures that cannot find for themselves, but Allah provides for them and you! (29:60)

Allah helps those who helps others.

The Opener
AL-FATTAH

"He is the All-deliverer, the All-knowing." (34:26)

Allah opens the stores of His mercy for people. Mercy can come in many different forms: guidance, knowledge, profit, substance and deliverance from evil and hardship. "Whatever mercy Allah bestows upon men, none can withhold, and whatever He withholds, none can bestow, apart from Him." (35:2)

Allah opens the hearts of the faithful to His knowledge. "Whoever Allah desires to guide, He opens his bosom to Islam." (6:125)

Allah opens the gates of forgiveness for the servants who repent. The Prophet, peace be upon him, told of a gate in the west, the width of which is forty years of travel, which is open for repentance and which will not close until the sun rises from it. (*Tirmidhi*)

A sincere propagator of

Islam will never despair. He will always hope that people will be guided. "Our Lord, give true deliverance between us and our people; You are the best of Judges" (7:89). "Say: 'Our Lord will bring us together and then judge rightly between us. He is the All-deliverer, the All-knowing." (34:26)

Al-Fattah is an intensive form of *al-Fatih* (the Deliverer, the Conqueror).

"Say:'Our Lord will bring us together and then judge rightly between us. He is the All-deliverer, the All-knowing." (34:26)

With Allah's help, a handful can conquer a multitude.

The All-knowing

AL-'ALIM

"Surely Your Lord, He is the All-creator, the All-knowing." (15:86)

Allah's knowledge is comprehensive. It extends to everything seen and unseen, present and future, near and far, existing and non-existing, His knowledge precedes, and is the cause of, existence. "With Him are the keys of the Unseen; none knows them but He. He knows what is on the land and in the sea; not a leaf falls, but He knows it. There is not a grain in the earth's shadows, not a thing, fresh or withered, but it is recorded in a glorious book." (6:59)

"Allah, alone has knowledge of the Hour of Doom; He sends down the rain; He knows what is in every womb. No soul knows what it shall earn tomorrow, and no soul knows in what land it shall die, Surely Allah is All-knowing and All-aware." (31:34)

Allah's knowledge of the most secretive thoughts is a basic creed in Islam. It is the cause of individual integrity: "And know that Allah knows what is in your hearts, so be fearful of Him." (2:235)

Compared to that, human knowledge seems insignificant. "Little indeed is the Knowledge vouchsafed to go." (17:85)

Allah is also called *Allam* (Much-knowing) and *Alim* (Knower). He is also called *Muhit* (Encompassing in knowledge). "Allah encompasses everything with His knowledge." (65:12)

"Little indeed is the Knowledge vouchsafed to go."
(17:85)

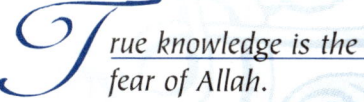

True knowledge is the fear of Allah.

AL-QABID

"It is Allah who encriches and makes poor. To Him you shall all return" (2:245). "Allah gives abundantly to whom He will, and sparingly to whom He pleases." (13:26)

Allah seizes souls in sleep and at death, "Allah takes men's souls at the time of their death, and the souls of the living during their sleep; He withholds those against whom He has decreed death, but sends the rest back for a stated term. (39:42)

The Prophet, peace be upon him, reported that Allah said, "I have never hesitated in putting into effect something I am to do in the way that I hesitate in seizing the soul of My faithful servant; he hates death and I hate to hurt him; yet it is inevitable." (*Al-Bukhari*)

Allah wards off evil from His servants. He says to Satan: "Surely over My true servants you shall have no authority! Your Lord suffices as a guardian." (17:65)

The Prophet said: 'Say, Allah, I have been an oppressor to myself. And there is no one but You who can forgive my sins. Therefore forgive me in Your generosity. And show me compassion. Verily, You are Forgiving and Compassionate.' (*At-Tirmidhi and Muslim*)

"Allah gives abundantly to whom He will, and sparingly to whom He pleases."
(13:26)

Patience is the best armour of the believer.

 The Expander
AL-BASIT

"Allah enriches and makes poor, and to Him you shall all return." (2:245)

Allah gives abundantly to whoever He will. "Allah extends His bounty and reduces His provision to whoever He will." (13:26)

"The Jews have said, 'Allah's hand is fettered.' May their own hands be fettered, and may they be cursed for what they have said. Nay, but His hands are both outspread; He bestows as He will." (5:64)

Allah extends His forgiveness to people all the time; all we have to do is ask for it. "Allah, Most High, stretches out His hands at night for the day sinner to repent, and He stretches out His hands in the day for the night sinner to repent, until the sun rises from the west." (*Muslim*)

A Muslim gives to charity, never fearing poverty. "Who will grant Allah a good loan? He will repay him many times over. Allah enriches and makes poor." (2:245)

It is a sign from Allah for people to reflect upon, that He spread the earth, though spherical in form, like a carpet. "And Allah has laid the earth for you as a carpet." (71:19)

Another fact which is scientifically significant is the way Allah, Most High, spreads clouds in the sky: "Allah is He that looses the winds, that stir up clouds, and He spreads them in heaven how He will, and scatters them; then thou seest the rain issuing from the midst of them." (30:48)

"Allah extends His bounty and reduces His provision to whoever He will." (13:26)

Be content with what Allah ordains.

AL-KHAFID

The Abaser

"Then We shall reduce him to the lowest of the low." (95:5)

Honour or abasement in this life are not final. Allah may raise people and abase others in order to put everyone to the test. "As for man, whenever his Lord tries him by honouring him, and blessing him, he says, 'My Lord has honoured me.' But when He tries him by grudging him His favours, he says, 'My Lord has despised me.'" (89:15-16)

But the real good and true honour come with the purification of the self. "By the soul and That which shaped it and enlightened it as to right and wrong: truly he succeeds who purifies it, and failed has he who corrupts it." (91:7-10)

If man rebels against Allah and pursues evil, his nature will be abased to the lowest possible position. "We indeed created Man in the best of moulds, then We made him the lowest of the low—save those who believe, and do righteous deeds." (95:4-6)

Those arrogant people who deny the unity of Allah are destroyed "so that We might let them taste the chastisement of degradation in the present life; and the chastisement of the world to come is even more degrading, and they shall not be helped." (41:16)

The Day of Judgment is described as "abasing, exalting" (56:3) because on that day truth will prevail and falsehood will be abased. Things will be really what they seem to be.

"By the soul and That which shaped it and enlightened it as to right and wrong: truly he succeeds who purifies it, and failed has he who corrupts it."
(91:7-10)

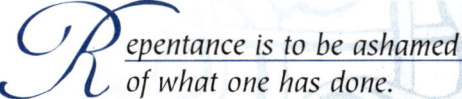

Repentance is to be ashamed of what one has done.

AL-RAFI'

The Exalter

"Allah will raise up in rank those of you who believe." (58:11)

Honour in the Kingdom of Allah comes with merit. There, rank is related to one's response to his Lord, and that depends on faith and knowledge,—true knowledge and insight. "Allah will raise up in rank those of you who believe and have been given knowledge." (58:11)

True exaltation comes with spiritual enlightenment. "Some there are to whom Allah spoke, and some He raised in rank." (2:253)

Prophethood is the highest position possible for mortals. "Such was Our argument, with which We furnished Abraham against his people. We raise up in degrees whom We will" (6:83). And Allah says to Muhammad, peace be upon him,: "Did We not give you high renown?" (94:4). Also, He says about Prophet Idris, peace be upon him, "He was a true man, a prophet. We raised him up to a high place." (19:56-57)

Elevation in this world and material success, if devoid of faith, are of no value. "Did he not know that Allah had destroyed before him generations of men superior to him in might, and more avaricious than he?" (28:78)

"Such was Our argument, with which We furnished Abraham against his people. We raise up in degrees whom We will." (6:83)

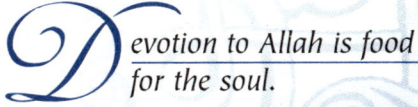

Devotion to Allah is food for the soul.

AL-MU'IZZ

The Honourer

"You exalt whom You will" (3:26).

Allah is *'Aziz*, Possessor of Glory, and *Mu'iz*, Giver of Glory. He gives glory to His obedient and loving servants. Glory, in the Islamic concept is not merely material power. It is the greatness of the soul that lives competently in this world, yet with its ultimate goal the Hereafter. "I will set your followers above the unbelievers till the Resurrection Day." (3:55) Allah gives material power to whoever He will. "You exalt whom You will, and You abase whom You will; in Your hand is the good" (3:26). But this sort of power is not always a reward; it could be a test: how would a powerful man behave? "But seek, amidst that which Allah has given you the Last Abode, and do not forget your portion of the present world; and do good, as Allah has been good to you" (28:77). Thus a believer's sense of pride and power, issues from his faith and the knowledge that Allah will always support him. "Surely We shall help Our Messengers and those who have believed, in the present life, and upon the day when the witnesses arise." (40:51)

"Surely We shall help Our Messengers and those who have believed, in the present life, and upon the day when the witnesses arise."
(40:51)

Self-seeking places one far from Allah.

AL-MUDHILL

The Humiliator

"And You humiliate whom You will." (3:26)

Allah humiliates those who disbelieve in or disobey Him. "Surely those who oppose Allah and His Messenger are among the most abject" (58:20). "So Allah lays His scourge upon the unbelievers." (6:125)

Humiliation may be theirs in this life. As for those who worship false gods, "their Lord's anger shall overtake them and abasement shall be their lot in this present life; thus do We recompense those who invent falsehoods" (7:152). Moreover, eternal disgrace will be their fate on the Day of judgement. "Shame and sorrow shall this day smite the unbelievers." (16:27)

Once a man is humiliated and disgraced by Allah, he will never be honoured. "He who is humbled by Allah has none to honour him" (22:18). This is what happened to the Jews:

"Abasement and humiliation were stamped upon them, and they were laden with the burden of Allah's anger, because they had disbelieved in the signs of Allah and slain His prophets unjustly." (2:61)

"He who is humbled by Allah has none to honour him."
(22:18)

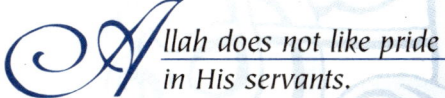

Allah does not like pride in His servants.

AL-SAMI'

The All-hearing

"Truly, Allah is All-hearing, All-seeing." (31:28)

Allah hears everything, nothing escapes His divine hearing, and no call prevents Him from hearing other calls. "Surely I shall be with you, hearing and seeing." (20:46)

Whether we speak loudly or quietly makes no difference to Allah. Some Muslims were journeying with the Prophet, peace be upon him, and they were praising Allah aloud. Then the Prophet said to them, "Quietly, for you are not calling someone deaf or absent; He is All-hearing, Close. The One you call is closer to each of you than the neck of his camel." (Al-Bukhari, Muslim)

Whatever we profess, or say aloud, conveys no information Allah. He knows not only our secrets, but also what we try to conceal in our hearts. "You have no need to speak aloud; for He knows all that is secret and all that is hidden." (20:7)

When we speak of Allah hearing and seeing, we do not imply that Allah has organs like those needed by human beings for cognitive functions. We believe that He hears and sees, but how is beyond our grasp.

"You have no need to speak aloud; for He knows all that is secret and all that is hidden."
(20:7)

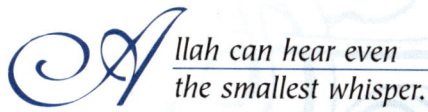

Allah can hear even the smallest whisper.

AL-BASIR

The All-seeing

"And He is the All-hearing, the All-seeing." (42:2)

Allah sees everything everywhere all the time. If we are always aware of that, we will be too shy to act foolishly or to commit sins. "Did he not know that Allah sees?" (96:14). "Surely Allah sees His servants" (40:44).

The feeling that someone important is looking at you makes you act in a noble way. To a believer, the most important One to see his doings is Allah and then those loved by Allah. "Say: 'Work; and Allah will surely see your work, and so will His Messenger, and the believers.'" (9:105)

If a believer develops this sense of being constantly present in front of Allah, he will certainly reach the rank of *Ihsan* (goodness, sincerity). Gabriel said to the Prophet, peace be upon him, "Tell me about *Ihsan*." The Prophet said, "It is to worship Allah as though you are seeing Him; and while you do not see Him, truly He sees you." (*Muslim*)

"Say:'Work; and Allah will surely see your work, and so will His Messenger, and the believers.'"
(9:105)

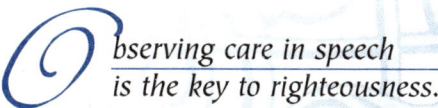

bserving care in speech is the key to righteousness.

The Judge

AL-HAKAM

"His is the Judgment, and to Him you shall all return." (28:88)

Allah is the Judge whose judgment is implemented and cannot be nullified. "Allah judges; none can reverse His judgment; He is swift in His reckoning" (13:41). Though things may sometimes seem out of control, believers must trust Allah's judgement. "And be patient until Allah shall judge; and He is the best of judges." (10:109)

Allah's judgement prevails in this life and in the hereafter. What passes unsettled here will be justly dealt with on the Day of Judgement (hence its name). "Then they are restored to Allah their true Protector. Surely His is the judgement; He is the swiftest of reckoners." (6:62)

The law given to us by Allah must not be altered or replaced: "What, shall I seek out any judge but Allah? For it is He who sent down to you the Book with all its precepts." (6:114)

We must accept Allah's decree loyally, not attempting to vie with Him in wisdom. "It is not for any believer, man or woman, when Allah and His Messenger have decreed a matter, to have any choice in his or her affairs. Whoever disobeys Allah and His Messenger has indeed strayed into manifest error." (33:36)

>
>
> *"Then they are restored to Allah their true Protector. Surely His is the judgement; He is the swiftest of reckoners."*
> *(6:62)*

Weigh up your actions before they are weighed up on the divine scales of justice.

 The Just
AL-'ADL

"Surely Allah enjoins justice and the doing of good." (16:90)

Allah is just in all His doings. He gives to each what he deserves, and puts everything in its proper position. "Surely Allah shall not wrong anyone by so much as the weight of an ant." (4:40)

Yet, to believe that Allah is the Just in spite of the grave injustices, perpetrated by human beings, which go unpunished in this world, is to truly believe in the Unseen. It is a test of faith; because when ultimate justice is fulfilled, it will be past the time of belief or disbelief—it will be the Day of Judgement: "We shall set up just balances on the Resurrection Day, so that not one soul shall be wronged in anything; even if it be by the weight of one grain of mustard-seed Our Reckoning shall suffice." (21:47)

Actions recorded in this life

will be judged on that Day; "This is because of the unrighteous deeds which your hands have sent on before you: for Allah is never unjust to His servants." (3:182)

There is nothing Allah hates more than injustice and transgression. "O My servants, I have forbidden oppression for Myself and have made it forbidden amongst you. So do not oppress one another." (*Muslim*)

"This is because of the unrighteous deeds which your hands have sent on before you: for Allah is never unjust to His servants."
(3:182)

Great and small weigh alike in the scales of Allah's justice.

AL-LATIF

The Subtle

"Allah is benign to His servants." (42:19)

Allah is gentle to people. He looks after them though they may not be aware of it. "Allah is benign to His servants, providing for whoever He will." (42:19)

'Al-Latif' also means 'the All-subtle.' Sometimes Allah's kindness comes in subtle ways; ways people may not discern. He may turn an anticipated calamity into a less harmful incident or even into a blessing. The Prophet Joseph, peace be upon him, had this to say when Allah turned his misfortunes to glory and happiness: "My Lord is gracious to whom He will." (12:100)

The All-Subtle is also the One who cannot be apprehended by any means, while He sees even those things that seem to us invisible, like vision itself. "No vision can grasp Him, but He has a grasp over all vision; He is the All-subtle, the All-aware." (6:103)

Thus our hearts and minds are open to Allah; He knows the most hidden thoughts and secrets. "Shall He who has created all things not know them all? And He is the All-subtle, the All-aware." (67:14)

This is the Name to call when one is in hardship, asking for Allah's gentleness and subtle intervention.

"Shall He who has created all things not know them all? And He is the All-subtle, the All-aware."
(67:14)

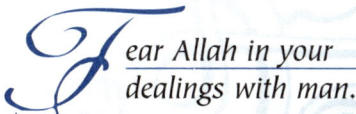

Fear Allah in your dealings with man.

The All-aware

AL-KHABIR

"And He is the All-subtle, the All-aware." (67:14)

Allah's knowledge is profound and comprehensive. He has the knowledge and the understanding of the Creator, the Maker. "Whether you speak in secret or aloud, He knows your inmost thoughts. Shall He who has created all things not know, them all? And He is the All-subtle, the All-aware" (67:13-14). "And Allah is aware of the things you do." (3:153)

Whatever sins one may commit, one will be answerable to Allah for them, even if Allah is the only witness. He has no need of other evidence. His knowledge and sight are all-sufficient. "Is he not aware that when that which is in the tombs is scattered abroad, and that which is in human breasts is brought out—surely on that day their Lord shall be aware of them?" (100:9-11). "Your

Lord suffices as one who is aware of and sees the sins of His servants." (17:17)

Whosoever of you sees an evil action, let him change it with his hand; and if he is not able to do so, then with his tongue; and if he is not able to do so, then with his heart, for that is the minimum that is desirable from a believer. (*An-Nasai*)

"Whether you speak in secret or aloud, He knows your inmost thoughts. Shall He who has created all things not know, them all? And He is the All-subtle, the All-aware."
(67:13-14)

Everything happens through the instrumentality of Allah.

AL-HALIM

The All-clement

"And know that Allah is All-forgiving, All-clement." (2:235)

Allah does not punish people for every sin. He tolerates the minor ones and postpones the punishment of some of the major ones, so that we may repent. "If a misfortune befalls you, it is the fruit of your own labours; and He pardons much." (42:30)

Allah is provoked neither by the disobedience nor the disbelief of people. "If Allah should take men to task for their evil-doing, He would not leave on earth one creature that crawls; but He reprieves them till a time ordained." (16:61)

As Allah is so lenient, Muslims should be lenient and tolerant with each other and with fellow human beings in general. Aisha, may Allah be pleased with her, said, "Allah's Messenger, peace be upon him, never took revenge for himself in any matter; but if a sanctity of Allah's was violated, he took revenge for Allah, may He be exalted." (*Al-Bukhari, Muslim*)

The Prophet, peace be upon him, said, to a companion. "You have two qualities that Allah loves: clemency and forbearance." (*Al-Bukhari, Muslim*)

Allah's clemency issues from His knowledge of our human weaknesses. "And surely Allah is All-knowing, All-clement." (22:59)

"If a misfortune befalls you, it is the fruit of your own labours; and He pardons much."
(42:30)

There is no limit to Allah's mercy.

AL-'AZIM

The All-glorious

"And He is the All-high, the All-glorious." (42:4)

Allah's reality is too great to be grasped by the human mind. He is infinitely greater than His creation. "Then magnify the Name of thy Lord: The All-glorious" (56:74). To magnify his Name we should repeat *Subhana rabbiyal Azim*, (Glory be to my Lord, the All-glorious).

Allah is so great that His Throne, which is the symbol of authority, comprises the heavens and the earth. "The preserving of them does not weary Him; He is the All-high, the All-glorious." (2:255)

As one feels the glory of the Creator, everything seems trivial, unworthy of sacrificing His good pleasure for it. The Prophet, peace be upon him, recommended that we keep saying these two phrases, "which are light on the tongue and dear to the All-merciful: Glory and praise be to Allah, glory be to Allah the All-glorious." (*Al-Bukhari, Muslim*)

And if one is in trouble, one should say, "There is no god but Allah, the All-glorious, the All-clement; there is no god but Allah, Lord of the seven heavens and of the Noble Throne." (*Al-Bukhari, Muslim*)

"The preserving of them does not weary Him; He is the All-high, the All-glorious." (2:255)

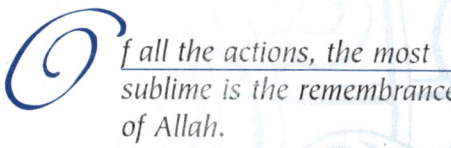

Of all the actions, the most sublime is the remembrance of Allah.

The Forgiving

الغَفُورُ
AL-GHAFUR

"Truly Allah is Oft-forgiving and All-compassionate." (2:173)

Allah's forgiveness is unlimited. "Tell My servants that I am the Oft-forgiving and the All-compassionate" (15:49). Knowing this, believers serve Allah with hope, not despair, in their hearts. "O My servants, you sin by night and by day, and I forgive all sins, so seek forgiveness of Me and I shall forgive you." (*Muslim*)

So, if one commits a sin, one should turn to his Lord in humility and repentance, and ask Him sincerely for forgiveness. "By the One in whose Hand is my soul! If you have not erred, Allah will have taken you and will have replaced you with people who err, then ask Allah, Most High, for forgiveness, and He forgives them." (*Muslim*)

The best way to pray for forgiveness is to say, "O Allah; You are my Lord. There is no god but You. You created me and I am Your servant, and I keep Your covenant and the promise I have made to You as far as I can. I seek refuge with You from the evil I have done. I attribute to You the blessings You have conferred on me and I confess my sins, so forgive me, for no one forgives sins but You." (*Al-Bukhari*)

"O My servants, you sin by night and by day, and I forgive all sins, so seek forgiveness of Me and I shall forgive you."
(Muslim)

The greatest favour to seek from Allah is forgiveness.

The Appreciative
AL-SHAKUR

"Surely Allah is All-forgiving, and bountiful in His rewards." (42:23)

Allah appreciates even the smallest of our acts of obedience and He rewards us for them in this life and the Hereafter. "Do not disregard any good deed, though it may be a smile on your face when you meet your brother." (*Muslim*)

Godly men do good hoping "for a commerce that will never fail, because Allah will give them their rewards, and will enrich them out of His bounty." (35:29-30)

Allah demands of His servants that they too should appreciate His generosity. "Be thankful for the blessing of Allah, if it be Him that you serve" (16:114). For, if they are grateful, i.e., if they acknowledge Him as the Giver of Bounty and use that Bounty to the best of their ability, Allah will enrich them. "If you are thankful, surely I will bestow abundance upon you." (14:7)

In return for our deeds with all their limitations, Allah gives eternal bliss. "But those who believe, and do righteous deeds, are the best of creatures; their recompense is with their Lord—the Gardens of Eden, watered by flowing streams, where they shall dwell for ever and ever. Allah is well-pleased with them, and they are well-pleased with Him." (98:7-8)

Shakur is the intensive of *Shakir* (Thankful) which is another Name of Allah.

"If you are thankful, surely I will bestow abundance upon you." (14:7)

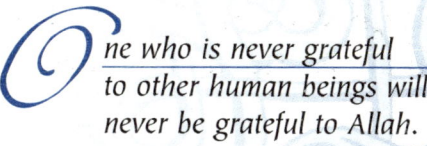

One who is never grateful to other human beings will never be grateful to Allah.

AL-'ALIY

The Sublime

"Allah is Exalted and Supreme." (4:34)

Allah is beyond any praise or description. "Glory be to the Lord of the heavens and the earth, the Lord of the Throne, above their falsehoods" (43:82).

No ordinary human being may claim to have seen or spoken to Allah, or to have the authority to speak for Him. Man is but a speck in Allah's creation. He is too low a creature to raise his eyes up to see his God. There are veils and veils between him and Allah, the All-high. Man is not fit to speak to Allah. Prophets, on the other hand, the last of whom is Muhammad, peace be upon them all, had this privilege. "It is not vouchsafed to any mortal that Allah should speak to him, except by revelation, or from behind a veil, or through a messenger sent and authorized by Him to make known His will. Surely He is Exalted and All-wise." (42:51)

Allah commands believers to "magnify the Name of your Lord the Most High," (87:1), and this they do many times in every prayer, repeating *"Subhana rabbiya'l-A'la"* (Glory be to my Lord, the Most High).

"Glory be to the Lord of the heavens and the earth, the Lord of the Throne, above their falsehoods."
(43:82)

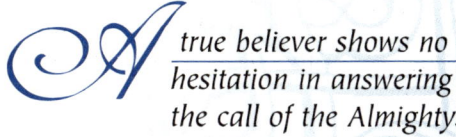

A true believer shows no hesitation in answering the call of the Almighty.

AL-KABIR — The Great

"The Knower of the unseen and the visible, the Supreme One, the Most High." (13:9)

Allah is great in Himself, His attributes and His actions. "Whatever else they invoke apart from Him is false; because Allah is the Most High, the Supreme One." (31:30)

In the heart of the believer, everything and every power, other than Allah, have no real value in themselves. Things must be weighed in terms of the good pleasure of Allah. All that displeases Him is invalidated. "We shall advance upon the work they have done, and render it as vain as scattered dust." (25:23)

A reminder of this is the Muslims' call for prayer: '*Allahu Akbar*' (Allah is great) which resounds five times a day all over the Muslim World. Any fear of any other being other than Allah or any hope for help, unless it be from Allah, must be cast aside.

Allahu Akbar is the *tasbih* (glorification) in the believer's heart and mouth. "O you, shrouded in your mantle, arise, and give warning. Glorify Your Lord." (74:1-3)

"We shall advance upon the work they have done, and render it as vain as scattered dust."
(25:23)

When man discovers the greatness of Allah, his own existence appears quite insignificant to him.

AL-HAFIZ

"My Lord is guardian over everything." (11:57)

Allah upholds the heavens and the earth and whatever is between them. "Allah holds the heavens and the earth, lest they fall." (35:41)

He also promised to safeguard the Holy Qur'an from change or from being perverted in meaning or forgotten, as was the case with the earlier Scriptures. "It is We who have sent down the Remembrance [the Qur'an] and We watch over it." (90:9)

People may forget or remember, but Allah knows the past, the present and the future. "The knowledge of them is with my Lord, in a Book; my Lord neither goes astray, nor forgets." (20:52)

Allah keeps a record of the deeds of every responsible person. He will call them to account for it. "We have neglected nothing in the Book;

then to their Lord they shall be mustered." (6:38)

If we put our trust in Allah, He will protect us. When Jacob entrusted Joseph to his other sons, he said: "Allah is the best guardian, and He is the most merciful of the merciful" (12:64). And the Prophet, peace be upon him, said: "Be mindful of Allah and He will protect you. Be mindful of Allah, and you will find Him in front of you" (*Tirmidhi*)

"We have neglected nothing in the Book; then to their Lord they shall be mustered."
(6:38)

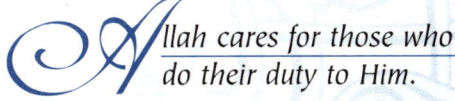

Allah cares for those who do their duty to Him.

The Sustainer
AL-MUQIT

"And Allah is the Sustainer of everything." (4:85)

Allah gives strength and diverse abilities to all His creatures. For every creature He provides the right sustenance: "And He blessed it (the earth) and ordained thereon its diverse sustenance in four days, for all alike." (41:10)

To provide food for everybody is no simple matter; to grasp the magnitude of the fact, consider only the number of all the species in existence and how they are preserved and balanced. "It is Allah who created the heavens and the earth, and sent down out of heaven water wherewith He brought forth fruits to be your sustenance" (14:32). "No creature is there crawling on the earth, but it is provided with sustenance by Allah." (11:6)

To Allah we owe the satisfaction of all needs, but He

is independent of all needs. "And He feeds all and is fed by none." (6:14)

A servant's heart is attached to Allah, seeking sustenance from Him only, and from no one else. "O My servants, all of you are hungry save those I have fed, so ask Me for food and I shall feed you. O My servants, all of you are naked save those I have clothed, so ask Me for clothing and I shall clothe you." (*Muslim*)

"And He blessed it (the earth) and ordained thereon its diverse sustenance in four days, for all alike."
(41:10)

Trust in Allah, not wealth.

The Reckoner
AL-HASIB

The Sufficient: "And Allah suffices as a reckoner." (33:39)

Whether we proclaim what is in our hears or hide it, Allah shall call us to account for it. "Truly, to Us they shall return; then upon Us shall rest their reckoning." (88:25-26)

There is not the smallest action, word or thought but must be taken account of by Allah. "Even if it be the weight of one grain of mustard-seed, We shall take it into account. Our reckoning shall suffice." (21:47)

So, our responsibility is to Allah, not to men. Men's opinions should have no bearing on our actions. Believers will always fear Him, "...... fearing none except Him; and Allah suffices as a reckoner." (33:39)

Al-Hasib also means the Sufficient. Allah alone is He who will and can discharge any trust reposed in Him. All other beings fail man and let him down. "Shall not Allah suffice His servant, though they frighten You with those they serve besides Him?" (39:36)

Thus, we call this Name when things go away and we need help.

>
>
> *"Shall not Allah suffice His servant, though they frighten You with those they serve besides Him?"*
> *(39:36)*

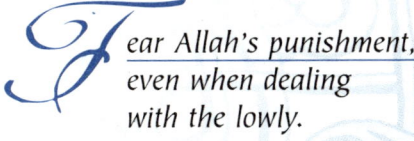

Fear Allah's punishment, even when dealing with the lowly.

AL-JALIL

The Majestic

"Thy Lord, Possessor of Majesty and Nobility." (55:27)

Allah is majestic and splendid. To Him is due all honour and devotion. "It is Allah I serve, with sincere devotion" (39:14).

Al-Jalil also means the One who is too great to be comprehended by human beings. Even the reflected glory of Allah is too great for the gross substance of matter. "'you shall not see Me; but behold the mountain—if it stays fast in its place, then you shall see Me.' And when His Lord manifested His glory on the mountain, He made it crumble to dust" (7:143).

Whenever we entreat on Lord, it is appropriate to call Allah by this Name: "O Possessor of Majesty and Nobility." (*Tirmidhi*)

O God, I seek divine guidance so that I may remain steadfast in what is just, I seek divine guidance in order to be firm in righteousness. I seek divine guidance in the manner that I express my gratitude for Your favours and worship with devotion. I seek from You a tongue that speaks the truth and a heart which is pure and clean. (*At-Tirmidhi*)

"It is Allah I serve, with sincere devotion."
(39:14)

Truly seeing the majesty of Allah, answers every problem.

AL-KARIM

The Generous

"My Lord is surely All-sufficient, All-generous." (27:40)

Allah has created for us all the things that are on earth. "And He subjected to you the night and day, and the sun and moon; and the stars are subjected by His command." (16:12)

His favours are showered on all,—the just and the unjust, the deserving and the undeserving. "Each We succour, these and those, from You Lord's bounty; and Your Lord's bounty is denied to none." (17:20)

Allah is most generous in rewarding good deeds. He gives in return manifold blessings. "Who is he that will lend Allah a good loan, and He will multiply it for him manifold?" (2:245)

This wonderful *hadith* shows us the extent of His benevolence: "He who has intended a good deed and has not done it, Allah records it as a good deed accomplished, but if he has intended it and has done it, Allah records it as if it were anything from ten good deeds to seven hundred good deeds—, or many times over." (*Al-Bukhari, Muslim*)

"Each We succour, these and those, from You Lord's bounty; and Your Lord's bounty is denied to none."
(17:20)

When man realises Allah's blessing upon him, his soul is filled with gratefulness to Him.

The Watchful
AL-RAQIB

"Allah is ever watchful over you." (4:1)

Allah is the Watchful One who never forgets what He has created, the Present One who is never absent. "Allah is watchful over everything." (33:52)

He is like a Guardian defending His Law, and protecting the weak and innocent. Allah's providence is ever vigilant; there is nothing hidden or unknown to Him. "He knows what comes into the earth, and what comes forth from it, what comes down from heaven, and what goes up into it. He is with you wherever you are; and Allah sees the things you do." (57:4)

Allah is ever on the watch, hearing and seeing, and all men are accountable to Him. This should caution His servants and make them fear His anger. "If three men conspire secretly together, but He is their fourth, if five men, He is their sixth;

whether fewer than that, or more, He is with them, wherever they may be." The point of all this is that, on the Day of Judgement, "He shall tell them what they have done" (58:7).

This is the name to call when one anticipates conspiracy and fears some violation of one's rights.

"He shall tell them what they have done."
(58:7)

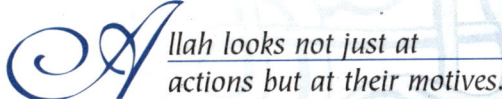

Allah looks not just at actions but at their motives.

AL-MUJIB

One Who Answers All

"Surely my Lord is near at hand and answers all." (11:61)

A believer is taught that Allah is very close to him and ready to answer his prayers. "And when My servants question you concerning Me—I am near to answer the call of the caller, when he calls to Me." (2:186)

He listens to the prayers of the righteous. "He answers those who believe and do righteous deeds and He enriches them through of His bounty." (42:26)

On the other hand, the disobedient man should not expect his prayer to be answered. The Prophet, peace be upon him, cites the man "who spreads out his hands to the sky [saying]:O Lord! O Lord! —while his food is unlawful, his drink unlawful, his clothing unlawful, and he is nourished unlawfully, and asks how he can be answered." (*Muslim*)

Allah listens to man's cry of agony and relieves his suffering. He is One "Who answers the distressed soul, when he calls to Him, and removes the evil and appoints you to be the inheritors of the earth?" (27:62)

So, whenever one stands helpless in the face of difficulties, one should call upon his Lord, even if it be for a very small matter. Allah loves to hear His servants calling Him. "Every night, when the last third of the night remains, our Lord, most exalted, descends to the lowest sky and says, "If there be anyone to call Me, I will answer him; if there be anyone to ask things of Me, and I will give them to him, and if there be anyone to ask for forgiveness, I will forgive him." (Al-Bukhari, Muslim)

> "Who answers the distressed soul, when he calls to Him, and removes the evil and appoints you to be the inheritors of the earth?"
> (27:62)

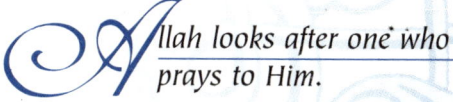

Allah looks after one who prays to Him.

AL-WASI'

The All-embracing

"And Allah is All-embracing, All-knowing." (2:247)

Allah's knowledge, mercy, forgiveness and provision are vast. Allah embraces all things in His knowledge. "If the sea were ink with which to write the Words of my Lord, the sea would be dried up before the Words of my Lord were finished." (18:109)

Allah is All-embracing in mercy. "And My mercy embraces all things, and I shall prescribe it for those who are god-fearing and pay the alms, and those who indeed believe in Our signs." (7:156)

He is All-embracing in forgiveness. "Surely Your Lord is generous in His forgiveness." (53:32)

And He is All-embracing in His provision. "O My servants! Were the first of you and the last of you, the human of you and the jinn of you to rise up in one place and make a request of Me, and were I to give everyone what he requested, that would not decrease what I have, any more than a needle decreases the sea if dipped in it." (*Muslim*)

"Surely Your Lord is generous in His forgiveness."
(53:32)

To know Allah is to know the one who knows everything there is to know.

AL-HAKIM

The Wise

"Surely Allah is Omniscient and All-wise." (9:28)

Wisdom, the pure essence of knowledge, is all Allah's; His designs in nature and life, are impeccable, perfect and absolutely accurate. His actions have purpose, none is pointless; His Revelation is full of light, wherein there is no crookedness; His creation is immaculate and in proportion. It is He "who has created all things well." (32:7)

What Allah does and says is always right, and there is meaning to it, whether we comprehend it or not. Allah assures us of this: "We did not create the heaven and the earth, and whatever is between them in sport." (21:16)

To glorify Him, we join the invokers in their call: "Our Lord, You have not created this out of vanity, Glory be to You" (3:191). True wisdom, which is the greatest gift to man, comes only from Allah: "He gives wisdom to whoever He will, and whoever is given wisdom, has been given much good" (2:269). And true wisdom is embodied in the Qur'an, the Magnificent Word of Allah, for it demonstrates the Oneness of Allah. "That is but part of the Wisdom Your Lord has revealed to you: set up with Allah no other god, or you will be cast into Hell, despised and rejected." (17:39)

"We did not create the heaven and the earth, and whatever is between them in sport."
(21:16)

The greatest intelligence is the least attachment to the world.

The Loving

الودُود
AL-WADUD

"And He is the Oft-forgiving, the All-loving." (85:14)

Wudd, the origin of Wadud, means "purest and finest love." Between Allah and His faithful servants there is such mutual love: "He loves them and they love Him" (5:54). He is well-pleased with them; He pardons, forgives and praises them.

To gain His precious love, they adhere to the ways of His Prophet, peace be upon him. "Say: "If you love Allah, follow me and Allah will love you."" (3:31)

They offer Him good deeds, deeds described in the revelation as being loved by Him. "The All-Merciful will cherish those who believe and do deeds of righteousness." (19:96)

When someone is loved by Allah, a wondrous thing happens to him. He is elevated to a very special position: that of a friend of Allah. All his deeds become those approved and blessed by Allah. "When I love him I am his hearing with which he hears, his seeing with which he sees, his hand with which he strikes, and his foot with which he walks. Were he to ask [something] of Me, I would give it to him." (*Al-Bukhari*)

Moreover, He makes Gabriel and the angels love Him. Human beings likewise will be made fond of Him.

This is the Name to call if you fear treachery or enmity; or if you want love and peace to spread among dear ones.

"The All-Merciful will cherish those who believe and do deeds of righteousness."
(19:96)

Allah's favourite servants are those of the finest character.

AL-MAJID

The Glorious

"Lord of the Throne, the All-noble." (80:15)

Al-Majid is another comprehensive Name that covers several attributes: He possesses perfect honour and nobility. He is the All-noble in Himself and His Doings. Being His Word, the Holy Qur'an is described as *"Majid"*: "By the Noble Qur'an!" (50:1).

Al-Majid has the further meaning of 'generous.' (See *Al-Karim*).

He is also the One who multiplies His blessings, spiritual and material: He increases them in quantity, and makes them better, and more lasting. So, Allah is praised by this Name where His blessings are solicited: "May the mercy of Allah and His blessings be upon you, O people of the House! Surely He is worthing of praise and glory." (11:73). And in every prayer we call Him by this Name, saying,

"You are All-laudable, All-noble," when we ask Allah to give Muhammad the mercy and blessings He gave to Ibrahim, peace be upon them both.

"May the mercy of Allah and His blessings be upon you, O people of the House! Surely He is worthing of praise and glory."
(11:73)

Rather from outward actions, greatness comes from inward grace.

AL-BA'ITH

The Resurrector

The Sender: "Allah shall raise up whoever is within the tombs." (22:7)

Our present form of life ends, yet death is but a phase after which Allah, the Resurrector, raises us and brings us to life again. "The unbelievers assert that they will never be raised up.

Say: 'Yes indeed, by my Lord! you shall be raised up, then you shall be told the things you did. That is easy for Allah'" (44:7).

Belief in the next life is crucial to our faith: what goes unpunished or unrewarded here will then be justly dealt with. We shall be raised so "that He may recompense those who have done evil according to their deeds and recompense those who have done good with what is best." (53:31)

Sleep, this mysterious phenomenon, is another form of

death. It is only by the will of Allah that we regain life when we wake up. "It is He who takes your souls by night, and He knows all that you have done by day; then He raises you up again." (6:60)

Al-Ba'ith also means 'the Sender': Allah sent messengers to convey truth to people and teach them, by the example of their own lives, how to lead a righteous life. "Indeed, We sent forth to every nation a Messenger, saying: 'Serve Allah, and eschew idols.'" (16:36)

'Yes indeed, by my Lord! you shall be raised up, then you shall be told the things you did. That is easy for Allah.'"
(44:7)

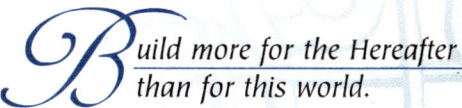

Build more for the Hereafter than for this world.

The Witness

AL-SHAHID

"And He is the witness of all things." (34:47)

There is nothing that we do but Allah is a witness to it. His knowledge not only comprehends all things, but is also neither subject to nor obliterated by time. "In whatever occupation you may be, and whatever portion you may be reciting from the Qur'an, and whatever deed you may be doing, We are witnesses to it when you are deeply engrossed in it." (10:61)

Allah is a witness to every activity in the universe: be it the words of a Messenger or the falling of raindrops. So, we are certain that no truth is ever lost. "Does it not suffice that Your Lord is the witness of all things?" (41:53)

Allah also suffices as a witness to the great fact that His Messengers spoke the truth: "Allah bears witness that what He has sent down to you,

He has sent with His knowledge; and the angels also bear witness; but Allah suffices for a witness." (4:166)

To be a witness implies being present at an event. Allah is never absent from any place, or at any time, but His presence is independent of such relative conceptions, which spring from of our limited human nature. "We shall relate to them [their whole story] with knowledge; assuredly We were never absent." (7:7)

"Does it not suffice that Your Lord is the witness of all things?"
(41:53)

Wrongful accusation is the worst of crimes.

AL-HAQQ

"And they shall know that Allah is the manifest Truth." (24:25)

Allah is the only Reality, so manifest, so high and so great. "He is the Truth, and what they invoke apart from Him—that is the false." (31:30)

He is the only True God and thus has every right to be worshipped. All other beings set up as deities are but shadows. "That then is Allah, your Lord, the True; what is there, after truth, but error? How then can you turn away from Him?" (10:32).

All His doings testify to this attribute: "It is He who created the heavens and the earth in truth" (6:73). We see in what true and perfect proportions all creation is held together.

He helps us find the truth. "Say: 'Allah—He guides to the truth,'" (10:35) and "Allah has sent down the Book with the truth." (2:176)

If people were to have a say in the running of the universe, its whole order would collapse. "Had the truth followed their caprices, the heavens and the earth and whoever dwelt therein would surely have been corrupted." (40:71)

The Prophet, peace be upon him, used to glorify his Lord, saying: "You are the Truth, Your saying is the truth, Your promise is the truth, Paradise is true, Fire is true, the Hour is true, the Prophets are true, and Muhammad is true." (*Al-Bukhari*)

"Had the truth followed their caprices, the heavens and the earth and whoever dwelt therein would surely have been corrupted."
(40:71)

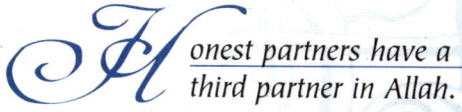

Honest partners have a third partner in Allah.

AL-WAKIL

The Trustee

"Allah suffices as a Disposer [of affairs]." (4:81)

Allah is All-good and All-powerful; all our affairs are best entrusted to His care, for He is the best Guardian of all interests; He is free of all the shortcomings that render human beings untrustworthy. "In Allah let the believers put all their trust." (3:160)

Putting one's trust in Allah means that one should take all possible precautions and then leave the results in the hands of Allah, who knows the working of events better than any human mind can conceive of. "When you are resolved, put your trust in Allah; surely Allah loves those who put their trust in Him" (3:159).

A true believer, like the Prophets, realizes that the fruition of his efforts comes only from Allah; therefore He turns to no one else for that.

With such a Disposer of

affairs to take care of him and of his well-being, the servant of Allah leads a life free of the burden of anxiety. "Allah is sufficient for us; He is an excellent Disposer [of affairs]." (3:173)

The Prophet, peace be upon him, recommended this prayer before sleeping: "*Allahumma*! I surrender myself to You; I turn my face to You; I commit my affairs to You; I rely on You, in hope and in fear of You; there is no shelter, no escape from You, except in You. I believe in Your Book that You revealed, and Your Prophet whom you sent." (*Al-Bukhari, Muslim*)

"I desire only to set things right, so far as I am able. My succour is only with Allah; in Him I have put my trust, and to Him I turn, in repentance."
(11:88)

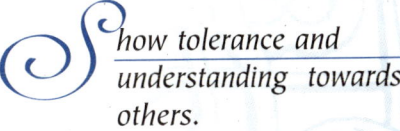

Show tolerance and understanding towards others.

AL-QAWIYY

The All-strong

"Your Lord is the All-powerful, the Almighty." (11:66)

Allah commands all power, it is all in His Hand. "There is no power except in Allah." (18:39)

Man's strength cannot be compared to that of Allah. For He is the Creator of all powers in the physical world, such as the wind, the rain and the living beings, and in the world of the unseen, hosts of angels execute the orders of their Lord. "To Allah belong the Forces of the heavens and the earth; and Allah is Almighty and All-wise." (48:7)

It happens that men get drunk with whatever power they may have obtained. They think that they are the mightiest beings. They wonder: "Who is mighter than we? What, did they not see that Allah, who had created them, was mighter than they?" (41:15)

But there will come a Day

when the strength of Allah will be displayed for all to witness. Alas, it will be too late to start to believe.

When they face their punishment the evil-doers will know. That might is Allah's alone." (2:165)

A promise is made by Allah to the believers that His strength will be on their side if they defend His Faith. "Allah has written, I shall assuredly be the victor. I and My Messengers. Surely Allah is Omnipotent and Almighty." (58:21)

"Who is mightier than we? What, did they not see that Allah, who had created them, was mightier than they?" (41:15)

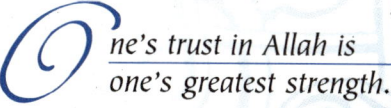

One's trust in Allah is one's greatest strength.

AL-MATIN

The Firm

"Surely Allah is the All-provider, the Possessor of strength, the Ever-sure." (51:58)

Allah's power is steadfast. It is the same today as yesterday, and will remain so forever. Stern is His might." (13:13)

Change does not apply to Him; nor to His Word: "My word cannot be changed," (50:29), nor to His creation; "There is no changing Allah's creation;" (30:30) nor to His Law: "And you will never find any change in the ways of Allah, and you will never find any diversion from His way of dealing." (35:43)

Allah's scheme for the evil-doers is unfailing. He allows them all the time they need, but His punishment is ready for them. "I grant them respite but assuredly My stratagem is sure." (7:183)

God's blessings are for everyone, but a strong believer

is better than a weak one. Wish for things which are beneficial to you, and in this, seek God's help. Do not lose heart, If you are visited by misfortune, do not say, 'If I had done this or that it could have been averted.' Because 'if' opens the door to Satan. (*Ibn Majah*)

"And you will never find any change in the ways of Allah, and you will never find any diversion from His way of dealing."
(35:43)

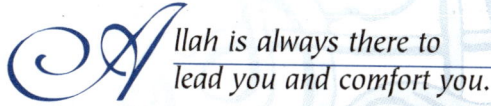

Allah is always there to lead you and comfort you.

The Protector

AL-WALIYY

"Allah—He is the Protector." (42:9)

Allah is the True Protector. He protects His servants from the powers of evil. "Allah is the Protector of the believers; He brings them forth from the darkness into the light." (2:257)

He supports them and grants them victory; He loves them, guides them and inspires them. Yet, some seek help from other beings whom they love and cherish apart from Allah; but the Quran tells them, "You have none, apart from Allah, as a protector and helper." (2:107)

If one loses the protection of Allah, no other power will be of any avail. "If Allah helps you, none can overcome you; but if He forsakes you, who then can help you?" (3:160)

Al-Waliyy is also "the Friend." Allah is the Friend of the god-fearing. "Surely my friend is Allah, who sent down the Book and who befriends the righteous." (7:196)

The believer's prayer is: "Appoint to us a protector from your presence, and appoint to us from Your presence a helper." (4:75)

"You have none, apart from Allah, as a protector and helper."
(2:107)

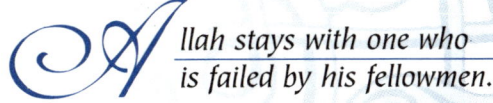

Allah stays with one who is failed by his fellowmen.

AL-HAMID

The Praiseworthy

"Surely Allah is All-sufficient, All-laudable." (14:8)

Allah is the only One who is Praiseworthy, for He has given us everything we enjoy in this life; even life itself. We should extol His favours, and love and exalt Him. "Praise be to Allah, the Lord of the heavens and the Lord of the earth, the Lord of all Being." (45:36)

The greatest gift for which Allah is to be praised is His revelations. Following their guidance, man achieves happiness in this world and the next.

"Praise be to Allah, who guided us thither, had Allah not guided us, we would surely have strayed from the right path. Indeed, our Lord's Messengers preached the truth." (7:43)

All creation, alive and inanimate, praises Allah and glorifies Him. "The seven heavens and the earth, and whoever is in them, extol Him;

There is nothing, that does not proclaim His praise, but you do not understand their extolling." (17:44)

We should join nature in this extolling and repeat *al-hamdu lillah* (praise be to Allah) which "fills the Balance [of good deeds]" (*Muslim*). In times of joy and in times of grief we should repeat these words.

A believer knows his own limitations. "I cannot duly praise you; You are as You have praised Yourself." (*Muslim*)

"Praise be to Allah, the Lord of the heavens and the Lord of the earth, the Lord of all Being."
(45:36)

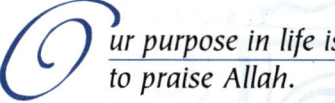

Our purpose in life is to praise Allah.

AL-MUHSI

The Reckoner

"He takes account of every single thing." (72:28)

Allah takes account of all things in the universe: their numbers, their movements and any changes that befall them. Tree leaves, sandgrains, and all higher and lower forms of life—what is now and what has vanished, are all counted and recorded. "Everything We have numbered in a Book." (78:29)

More important is the record Allah keeps of our deeds; even each breath we take is counted. A clear record of our life is preserved which will be set before us on the Day of Judgment: no omissions and no false entries. The evil-doers will be appalled at the exactitude of their registers. "Woe to us, what can this Book mean? It leaves out nothing, small or great. Everything is noted down." (18:49)

Further accounts will be produced by the different parts

of their bodies: "There shall be a woeful punishment in the day when their tongues, their hands and their feet shall testify to what they did." (24:24)

All this is to convince us that it is a fair trial, for Allah's knowledge is perfect, and independent of records. He 'knows' everything, while the actual writing down of our actions is performed by angels.

Allah says, "O My servants, it is but your deeds that I reckon up for you and then recompense you for, so let him who comes upon good praise Allah, and let him who comes upon the reverse blame no one but himself." (*Muslim*)

"Surely there are over you noble watchers, writers, who know whatever you do."
(82:10-12)

Be punctilious in paying people their dues.

AL-MUBDI

The Originator

"Surely it is He who originates and restores to life." (85:13)

Allah is the Originator of all creation. Nothing exists of its own accord. His will is the source of all being.

Allah's creative activity never diminishes. He is always originating things. Worlds are created and transformed every minute, worlds within our vision and worlds beyond our vision "And He has created things beyond your knowledge." (16:8)

We must understand that the world coming into being is a great sign of the Power and Unity of the Creator. "Say:'Journey in the land, then behold how He originated creation.'" (29:20)

Allah, most exalted, gives a hint as to how the process of creation began. "Have not the unbelievers beheld how the heavens and the earth were one solid mass, and how We tore it asunders, and We made every living thing from water?" (21:30). These are facts which our 'scientific' age is better able to appreciate, but does it touch the hearts of the faithless?

"Say:'Journey in the land, then behold how He originated creation.'"
(29:20)

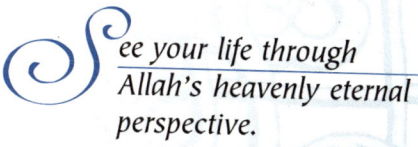

See your life through Allah's heavenly eternal perspective.

AL-MU'ID

The Restorer

"Surely it is He who originates and restores to life again. (85:13)

On Resurrection Day, Allah recreates us and brings us back to life, as responsible beings, to be confronted with the consequences of our doings on this earth. "Allah originates creation, then repeats it; then you shall all be returned to Him." (30:11)

The sceptical human mind may doubt the fact, yet the answer is very simple: "Just as We originated the first creation, so shall We produce a new one:—a promise binding on us; Truly, We shall fulfill it" (21:104).

The unbelievers go on arguing obstinately: "They say, 'What, when we are reduced to bones and dust, shall we really be raised up again in a new creation?' Say, 'Let you be stones, or iron, or some creation yet more monstrous in your minds! (Yet you will be raised up).' 'Then they will say,' 'Who will bring us back?' Say, 'He who first created you.'" (17:49-51)

Whenever a believer is striken with any hardship, or pain, or anxiety, or sorrow, or harm, or distress—even if it be a thorn that has hurt him—Allah redeems thereby some of his failings. (*Al-Bukhari, Muslim*)

"Allah originates creation, then repeats it; then you shall all be returned to Him."
(30:11)

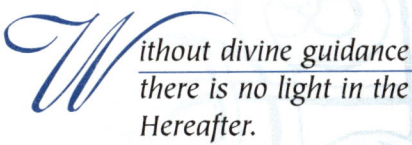

Without divine guidance there is no light in the Hereafter.

AL-MUHIYY

The Giver of Life

"Surely He is the Quickener of the dead." (30:50)

Allah is the Quickener: the Giver of life. It is He who bestows life on dead matter: Adam was made out of clay, then Allah breathed His spirit into him. "It is We who ordain life and death and to Us all shall return." (50:43)

Nature dies in winter; the earth, trees and seeds, all look lifeless; yet, "Behold the marks of Allah's mercy, how He quickens the earth after it was dead." (30:50)

Allah gives life back to the dead. That second life, whether happy or miserable, will be eternal. "It is He who gave you life, then He shall make you dead, then He shall give you life" (22:66). Allah is the giver of a much higher sort of life; besides the physical, He gives spiritual life. A man's life is meaningless if his soul is in oblivion. Allah's Word has the wonderful effect of rain on dry land: it brings forth life, beauty and fruitfulness. "Can he who was dead, to whom We gave life, and a light to walk by among men, be like him who is in the depths of darkness, from which he can never come out?" (6:122)

"Behold the marks of Allah's mercy, how He quickens the earth after it was dead."
(30:50)

Meet the challenge of a crisis with Allah's word, prayer, and praise to Him.

AL-MUMIT

The Life-taker

"It is He who grants life and death." (53:44)

Allah, who gives life, is the One who takes it. His Hand is behind all causes of death. "We have decreed Death to be your common lot; and We shall not be frustrated." (56:60)

Death to a Muslim is not the end of life, it is a transformation of it. He looks forward to meeting His Lord, because he believes in Him and in His good promises.

If death is decreed by Allah, the Omnipotent, then there can be no escape from it. "Wherever you may be, death will overtake you, even if you are in high, strongly built towers." (4:78)

So, cowardice and fear of death are meaningless. "Flight will not profit you, if you flee from death or slaughters." (33:16)

Allah withholds death from the people in Hell when they

cry for it, hoping it will end their agony. "Whoever comes to His Lord as a sinner, for him awaits Hell wherein he shall neither die nor live." (20:74)

The Prophet, peace be upon him, used to say at bedtime: *"Allahumma*! In Your Name I live and in Your Name I die." (*Al-Bukhari*)

"We have decreed Death to be your common lot; and We shall not be frustrated."
(56:60)

Truly destitute are those bereft of Allah's grace in the Hereafter.

AL-HAYY

The Living

"He is the Living One." (40:65)

Allah is the Living One whose Life is perfect; He is not subject to death or sickness, and is not dependent on any circumstances.

The Perfect Life comprises all attributes of perfection: perfect hearing, perfect seeing, perfect knowledge, etc. There can be only one such life: "There is no god but He, the Living, the Eternal." (3:2)

Allah is the only source and constant support of life in the universe. It is literally impossible for any other being to create life, because they have no control over any life, not even their own. "They have no power to cause death or give life or resurrect." (25:3)

A believer realizes that and attaches himself to the Living One. "Put your trust in the Living God, the Undying, and proclaim His praise." (25:58)

Allah's Life is not like ours.

It is absolute, self-subsisting and eternal. Life and death in this world as we know them are natural phenomena decreed to suit His plan and purpose of the creation. He "created death and life, so that He might try which of you is best in his conduct." (67:2)

>
>
> *"They have no power to cause death or give life or resurrect."*
> (25:3)

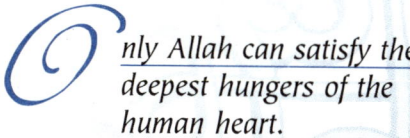

Only Allah can satisfy the deepest hungers of the human heart.

AL-QAYYUM

The Eternal

"Allah—there is no god but He, the Living, the Eternal." (2:255)

Al-Qayyum is one of the greater names that cover a host of meanings. In combination with other names (as in the verse above) it is thought to make the Greatest Name— *Al-Ism al-A'zam*.

Allah is the Eternal: the One without beginning or end, Absolute, not limited by time or place or circumstance.

He does not die nor does He need to rest or sleep. "Slumber does not seize Him and neither does sleep" (2:255). He never gets tired. "In six days We created the heavens and the earth, and all that lies between them, and We felt no weariness" (50:38)

Al-Qayyum is the One who exists by Himself, who is self-subsisting. He is also the One who keeps us and maintains the universe and all forms of life in it. "And one of His signs is that the heaven and the earth stand firm at His command." (30:25)

He looks after His creation, provides for it, and stands Guardian and is Watchful over it: It is He "who stands over every soul and all its actions." (13:33)

We are advised by the Prophet, peace be upon him, to call this Name as often as possible, especially when one is nearest to Allah, i.e. in prostration. He used to call, *"Ya Hayyu, ya Qayyum."* (O Eternal One, O Living One).

"And one of His signs is that the heaven and the earth stand firm at His command." (30:25)

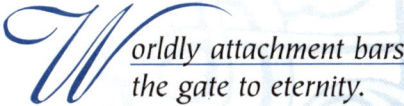

orldly attachment bars the gate to eternity.

AL-WAJID

The Finder

"Did He not find you needy, and enrich you?" (93:8)

Allah is the One who always finds whatever He wills and desires. He is in need of nothing.

He is the One whose bounty is inexhaustible, forever ready to be given. Human beings may not find anything in their possession worth giving, if they desire to give; but He always finds what is appropriate. "To Him belong the keys of the heavens and the earth." (42:12)

Allah is the Finder of truth, the True Knower. *Wijdan* means immediate, inner knowledge. "Did He not find you an orphan, and shelter you? Did He not find you erring, and guide you?" (93:6-7)

He knows the truth about our hearts. Some He finds bad: "We found the greater part of them untrue to their commitments; indeed, We found most of them sunk in evil ways" (7:102), And some He finds good: "Surely we found him a good and steadfast man." (38:44)

Al-Wajid also means the One who causes things to exist and happen; even our deeds are caused by the free will with which He has endowed us. "Say: 'Everything is from Allah.'" (4:78)

"Surely we found him a good and steadfast man."
(38:44)

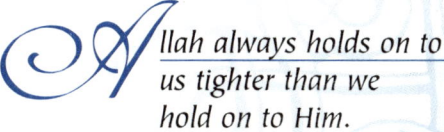

Allah always holds on to us tighter than we hold on to Him.

The Noble

AL-MAJID

"O Worthy of praise and nobility." (*Muslim*)

Allah is the Noble One, and the extremely Generous One, who gives abundantly; and this entitles Him to be glorified, praised and honoured.

His generosity is consistent and endless, for His wealth is endless. "Allah's Right Hand is full. Giving, night and day, never empties It. Do you see what He has given since he created the heavens and earth? It has not diminished what is in his Right Hand." (*Al-Bukhari, Muslim*)

In his prayer, the Prophet, peace be upon him, used to say: "Allahumma! Our Lord! Praise be Yours, [praise] that fills the heavens and the earth, and that fills whatever You desire beyond that; O worthy of praise and nobility!" (*Muslim*)

Majid and *Majeed* have the same root, *Majid* being in the intensive. Such repetition implies that the idea is wholly and exclusively the privilege of Allah.

God is bountiful and feels unhappy if He has to refuse to grant a wish. He feels embarrassed when a man holds out both his hands before Him, and He has to disappoint him by turning him away empty-handed. (*Abu Dawud, At-Tirmidhi*)

"Allahumma! Our Lord! Praise be Yours, [praise] that fills the heavens and the earth, and that fills whatever You desire beyond that; O worthy of praise and nobility!"
(Muslim)

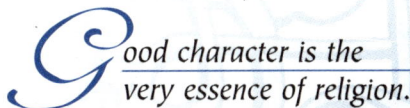

Good character is the very essence of religion.

AL-WAHID

"Allah is but One God." (4:171)

He is the One and Only God. There is no alternative to Him, no equal, no like, no partner, no son and no wife; He is above all such relationships. "He has not begotten, and has not been begotten, and none is equal to Him." (112:3-4)

Allah's qualities and nature are unique. What applies to human beings does not apply to Him. Attributing human qualities to the Creator has always corrupted people's concept of God. "What, has your Lord favoured you with sons and Himself adopted daughters from among the angels? Surely that is a monstrous thing to say!" (17:40)

Unity in Design and harmony in the universe proclaim the Unity of Will, and the Oneness of the Maker. "Allah has never begotten a son, nor is there any god besides Him; for then each god would have taken away what he had created and some would have risen up over others" (23:91)

"Do not wittingly set up other gods beside Allah," (2:22). According to the Islamic concept, any power man obeys apart from Allah is an equal to Allah set up by him. "Your God is One God, so surrender yourselves to Him." (22:34)

"He has not begotten, and has not been begotten, and none is equal to Him."
(112:3-4)

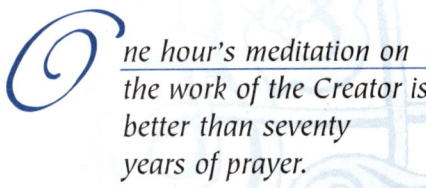

One hour's meditation on the work of the Creator is better than seventy years of prayer.

AL-SAMAD

The Everlasting Refuge

"Allah, The Everlasting Refuge." (112:2)

Allah is the Refuge sought by all persons in times of need. When in trouble, or distress, or facing adversity, man realizes that he is helpless and so turns to the source of all goodness and mercy. "When evil befalls mankind, they call to their Lord, turning to Him." (30:33)

And Allah is there, never failing, ready to answer the call of anguish: "Allah delivers you from them and from every distress; yet you worship false gods." (6:64)

If man seeks deliverance of beings other than Allah, he is betraying his trust in Him. "Call on those you defied apart from Him; they have no power to relieve your affliction, nor can they change it." (17:56). This does not alter the fact that Allah is the only Refuge. Man is the only loser if he ignores it.

Allah, may He be exalted, said: "I am as My servant thinks of Me, and I am with him if He calls me." (*Al-Bukhari, Muslim*). The good servant thinks and believes that He is the Refuge, the One who Answers and the Protector. "When you ask, ask Allah; and when you seek help, seek it of Allah." (*Tirmidhi*)

"Allah delivers you from them and from every distress; yet you worship false gods."
(6:64)

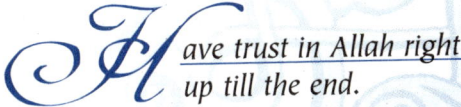

Have trust in Allah right up till the end.

AL-QADIR

"Say, 'He is the Powerful One.'" (6:65)

Allah has the power to do whatever He will. "When He decrees a thing, He need only say: 'Be', and it is" (36:82); and "Allah creates whatever He pleases. He has power over all things." (24:45)

Nothing can interfere in the designs of Allah, for "Allah's decrees are pre-ordained" (33:38); nor can anyone escape His judgment, for "there is naught in the heavens or the earth that can frustrate Him." (35:44)

Man should know that after a dead man turns to dust, "He is able to bring him back upon the day when all things secret are tested, and he shall have no strength, no helper." (86:8-10)

Realizing that we are capable of nothing ourselves, we must ask Him to give us strength. "*Allahumma*! I consult You for Your knowledge, I seek power from You, and I ask You for Your great bounty; for You are able and I am not, and You know and I do not; You are the Knower of things unseen." (*Al-Bukhari*)

Qadir also means 'Determiner' "We determine (according to need), for excellent determiners are We." (77:23)

Qadir, the intensive of *qadir,* is another Name of Allah.

"Allah creates whatever He pleases. He has power over all things."
(24:45)

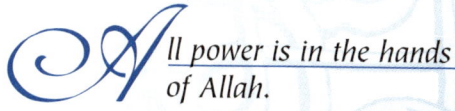

All power is in the hands of Allah.

AL-MUQTADIR

The Prevailing

"In the presence of a king All-powerful." (54:55)

Allah is the All-powerful who has absolute power and mastery. Nothing is beyond His power.

Al-Muqtadir and *Al-Qadir* both denote power, but *Al-Muqtadir* gives the further idea that the mastery arises from Allah's own nature, and it is absolute and general, not related to a specific task. "Allah has power over all things." (18:45)

Allah shows the extent of His Omnipotence by the acts of which He is capable; "Even if we take you away, We shall take vengeance upon them, or We shall show you what We promised them; surely We shall prevail over them." (43:41-42)

When His retribution was meted out to the obstinate disbelieving nations, it was a mighty and complete punishment. "They rejected all of Our signs; so We smote them with the scourge of the Mighty One, the All-powerful." (54:42)

Love for the life of this world is damaging to the life of the Hereafter. Anyone who values the life of the Hereafter will be indifferent to the life of this world. Therefore, prefer that which is eternal to that which is ephemeral. (*Ahmad Ibn Hanbal*)

"They rejected all of Our signs; so We smote them with the scourge of the Mighty One, the All-powerful."
(54:42)

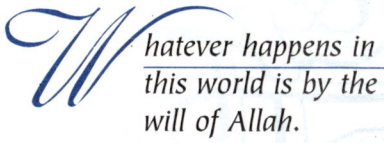

Whatever happens in this world is by the will of Allah.

AL-MUQADDIM

The Promoter

"You are the Promoter." (Al-Bukhari, Muslim)

Allah promotes to higher positions the servants whom He loves for being the staunchest in faith, and gives them a rich reward. "And those foremost in faith will be the ones brought nearest to Allah." (56:10-11)

In this life, however, Allah chooses to arrange people and matters as He wishes and for a purpose known only to Him; "We have apportioned to them their livelihood in the present life, and raised some of them above others in rank, so that some of them may take others into their service; and Your Lord's mercy is better than all their hoarded treasures." (43:32)

Allah conveys a warning to mankind, clear and strong, through His Messengers, showing them the path to incuring His anger and the path to earning His good pleasure. "Do not dispute before Me! For I sent you warning in advance." (50:28)

The Prophet, peace be upon him, used to say in prayer: "*Allahumma!* Forgive me the former and the latter [of my trespasses], what I have made secret and what I have declared, all my transgressions and all that You know better than I do. You are the Promoter and You are the Detainer. There is no god but You," (*Al-Bukhari, Muslim*).

"Do not dispute before Me! For I sent you warning in advance."
(50:28)

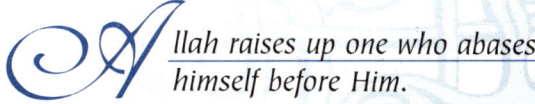

Allah raises up one who abases himself before Him.

The Detainer

AL-MU'AKHKHIR

"And You are the Detainer." (*Al-Bukhari, Muslim*)

Allah, most exalted, detains the unbelievers on the Day of Judgment, and keeps them at a distance from His Forgiveness and Mercy. "We swept the evildoers away like withered leaves." (23:41)

This is a just punishment because, when His Light has come to them in the Messages of the Prophet, they have stayed far away from it: "Those who do not believe are deaf and blind; they are like men who are called from a far off place." (41:44)

In this life people are sometimes detained and held back, by the will of Allah, from attaining whatever they want whenever they want. The timing of events is His privilege. Most important of all is the timing of the person's death. "Your day is already appointed. You cannot put it back by a single hour, nor put it forward." (34:30)

When the evil-doers are chastised and they know that their end has come, they cry to their Lord, "Our Lord, grant us respite for a while, and we will answer Your call, and follow Your Messenger." (14:44)

Allah may indeed choose to give respite; but it is for Him alone to give it; no other authority can alter His terms or modify them. "We shall defer it, save till the appointed hour." (11:104)

"Your day is already appointed. You cannot put it back by a single hour, nor put it forward."
(34:30)

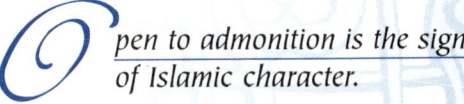

Open to admonition is the sign of Islamic character.

#

AL-AWWAL

"He is the First." (57:3)

Allah is the Being whose existence is without a beginning, for if there were a beginning for Him, then something should have caused Him to be, and that something should have existed before Him.

The Prophet, peace be upon him, said, "Allah has existed and [there was a time when] nothing other than Him existed" (*Al-Bukhari*). Allah indisputably preceded all beings in existence, and He is the Cause of their existence.

What we understand as 'before' and 'after' applies only to our circumstances: we live in time, governed by it, and we think in terms of beginnings and ends. But Allah is not governed by our time. We are told that "each day of your Lord is like a thousand years in your reckoning" (22:47), and also of "a day whose length is fifty thousand years." (70:4)

The Prophet, peace be upon him said, "Some men will go so far as to say, 'Allah created all creation; but who created Him?' Answer them thus, 'I believe in Allah and His Messengers.'" (*Muslim*)

This is a clear order not to discuss such matters; the human mind is too narrow to grasp the greatness of Allah.

"Allah has existed and [there was a time when] nothing other than Him existed."
(*Al-Bukhari*)

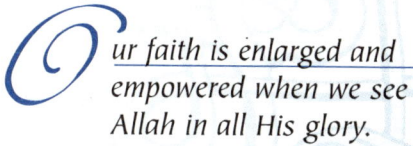

Our faith is enlarged and empowered when we see Allah in all His glory.

AL-AKHIR

The Last

"He is the First and the Last." (57:3)

Being the First and the Last shows that time is just another phenomenon created by Allah. He controls it and is not controlled by it. The Last is the Eternal one who will continue to exist after the universe as we know it, has vanished. "When the sight is dazed, and the moon eclipsed, and the sun and moon are brought together, upon that day man shall ask, 'Whither shall I flee?' But there shall be no refuge. Upon that day recourse shall be to Your Lord." (75:7-12)

The following is a beautiful supplication made by the Prophet, peace be upon him: "Allahumma! Lord of the seven skies and Lord of the earth, Lord of everything, Splitter of the grains and the date-stones, Sender of the Torah, the Gospel and the Qur'an, I take refuge with You from the evil of every evil-being that You take by the forelock. You are the First, so nothing is there before You; and You are the Last, so nothing is there after You. You are the Victor, so nothing is there beyond You. Pay my debts for me, and guard me against poverty." (*Muslim*)

>
>
> *'Whither shall I flee?' But there shall be no refuge. Upon that day recourse shall be to Your Lord."*
> *(75:7-12)*

No matter how wonderful life may be, eternal life will be infinitely better.

AL-ZAHIR

The Victor. The Outward. "He is the First and the Last, the Evident and the Immanent." (57:3)

Allah is the Evident, the Manifest. He made Himself evident without being visible. His doings tell us plainly about His existence and qualities: nature is rich in Signs all pointing to his Omnipotence; the wondrous making of man is another piece of evidence. "We shall show them Our signs in the horizons and in themselves, till it is clear to them that it is the truth." (41:53)

Allah's being is so evident that man's intrinsic nature, if uncorrupted, recognizes Him. No pure good soul can fail to hear in its inner being the call to the Unity of Allah: "Therefore, stand firm in your devotion to the true faith—the upright Faith which Allah created for man to embrace." (30:30)

Al-Zahir is also the Victor who is above all in might and exaltedness. He will proclaim His Word in the world. "It is He who has sent His Messenger with guidance and the religion of truth, so that He may uplift it above every religion, though the unbelievers be averse" (9:33). So, Islam, as the final and complete truth, will prevail.

"Therefore, stand firm in your devotion to the true faith—the upright Faith which Allah created for man to embrace."
(30:30)

Morality requires a base and there is no base except belief in Allah.

AL-BATIN

The Hidden

"He is the First and the Last, the Evident and the Immanent" (57:3). Allah is the Immanent; His Self and Reality are utterly unknown to us. The utmost knowledge we have of Allah is the realization of the impossibility of visualizing Him. "You are the Immanent, so there is nothing beyond You." (*Muslim*)

Also, the realm of the Unseen is the exclusive preserve of the Immanent. "He alone knows what is hidden and He does not disclose His secrets to anyone." (72:26)

The two Attributes, the Evident and the Immanent, show that Allah encompasses and transcends place and space, appearance and reality, just as the First and the Last encompass time. Allah comprehends all aspects of all matters: the outward, *al-Zahir*, and the inward, *al-Batin*.

His blessings too have two aspects; He "has lavished on you

His blessings both, outward and inward." (31:120)

Knowledge also has two aspects. "They know the outward show of the present life, but of the Hereafter they are heedless." (30:7)

Hence, inward knowledge is that which is related to faith and god-fearingness.

"They know the outward show of the present life, but of the Hereafter they are heedless."
(30:7)

Allah's love and forgiveness brings the only lasting peace to our soul.

AL-WALI

The Protector

"Apart from Him they have no protector." (13:11)

Allah is the Owner of things and beings, who disposes of them as He will, and whose judgment is immediately implemented.

Allah is also Al-Mawla, the Patron. Attributed to Allah, this means the Creator, the Provider, the Resurrector and the Owner. "Hold fast to Allah; He is your Patron—an excellent Patron, an excellent Helper." (22:7)

Allah guards those who struggle in His cause, and He watches over their interests closely and constantly. "Surely We shall help Our Messengers and those who have believed, in the present life, and upon the day when the witnesses arise." (40:51)

This is due to them from Allah, "because Allah is the Patron of the believers: the unbelievers have no patron." (47:11)

Be mindful of God and God will protect you. Be mindful of God and you will find Him before you. If you ask, ask of God; if you seek help, seek help of God. Know that if all the people were to gather together to give you the benefit of anything, it would be something that God had already prescribed for you, and that if they gathered together to harm you with anything, this would only be as God had already ordained. (*At-Tirmidhi*)

"Surely We shall help Our Messengers and those who have believed, in the present life, and upon the day when the witnesses arise."
(40:51)

When the storms of life get you down, open your spiritual eyes and see Allah at work.

AL-MUTA'ALI

The All-exalted

"The Knower of the unseen and the visible, the Supreme One, the Most High." (13:9)

Allah is high above His creation in power and authority, not in place or direction. Angels and worshippers look up to Him in awe and reverence. "They fear their Lord above them, and they do what they are commanded." (16:50)

So, observing His commands is the proof of submission: disobedience to them implies the disruption of this relationship. "Do not rise up against Allah; behold, I come to you with clear authority." (44:19)

All anthropomorphic elements are eliminated from the concept of God in Islam. Any tendency to conceive an image of Him is negatived, although unbelievers, of all persuasions and times, have associated other beings with Him, or invented images and attributed them to

Him. But "High indeed be He exalted above that they say!" (17:43)

He is exalted above the imperfection of having favourites (apart from the Chosen Prophets). "He—Exalted be our Lord's majesty!—has not taken to Himself either consort or a son" (72:3). Every human being enjoys His cherishing care, and can earn His love and mercy by following His Straight Path.

"Do not rise up against Allah; behold, I come to you with clear authority."
(44:19)

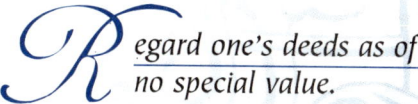

Regard one's deeds as of no special value.

AL-BARR

The Beneficent

"Surely He is the All-benign, the All-compassionate." (52:28)

Allah is the Benign One to His servants. He "desires ease for you; and does not desire hardship for you." (2:185)

He is Good to people; bestowing upon them health, wealth, honour, posterity and power. "Whatever blessing you have, it comes from Allah." (16:53)

Have the false gods that people have set up beside Him the power to give any of these things? "What, is Allah more worthy, or those that they associate with Him?" (27:59). There can be no doubt: "Allah is better and more abiding." (20:73)

Allah is specially benign to His faithful servants, for he chooses them as friends. He gives them greater faith, and the strength they need to serve Him; then He rewards them and forgives their sins. "Such are those from whom We shall accept the best of what they have done, and We shall pass over their evil deeds." (46:16)

He is the source of all the benignity and good feelings that bind the hearts of people together.

Al-Barr is also the Truthful One who fulfils His promises and executes His oaths. "We have come to You with the truth, and assuredly We are truthful." (15:64)

"Allah is better and more abiding."
(20:73)

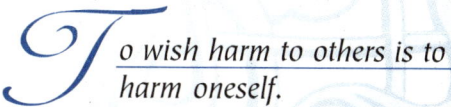

To wish harm to others is to harm oneself.

The Acceptor of Repentance

AL-TAWWAB

"Surely He is the Oft-returning" (2:37). Allah returns to His servant the favour of His mercy if he turns to the straight path and eschews the wrong course. "Such as repent and make amends, and make known the truth—towards them I shall turn; I am the Oft-returning, the All-compassionate." (2:160)

Man's nature is weak, and he may have to turn again and again to Allah for mercy. Allah is lenient and He accepts the regretful servant's repentance, if he is sincere. "It is He who accepts repentance from His servants, and pardons evil deeds." (42:25)

Not only does Allah accept repentance, but He is also extremely happy with it.

"Allah is happier with the repentance of His servant than anyone of you on finding his camel after he has lost it in a desert." (*Al-Bukhari, Muslim*)

Allah helps the individual

to repent; when he is depressed, heavy with guilt, and eager for a ray of hope, Allah guides him to declaring his repentance. "When the earth became constrained for them, for all its breadth, and their souls seemed straightened, and they thought that there was no shelter from Allah except in Him, then He turned towards them, so that they might repent." (9:118)

The Prophet, peace be upon him, said, "O people! Repent to Allah and ask Him for forgiveness; for I repent a hundred times a day." (*Muslim*)

"It is He who accepts repentance from His servants, and pardons evil deeds."
(42:25)

Allah gives us supernatural strength to walk the path He has chosen for us.

 The Avenger

AL-MUNTAQIM

"We shall take vengeance upon the sinners." (32:22)

Allah is very patient; He gives many opportunities to the worst sinners for repentance. But, eventually, there comes a time when justice must be done and punishment must be given: "So, when they had angered Us, We took vengeance on them, and We drowned them all together." (43:55)

Many nations were destroyed when they did not heed Allah's warning: those of the Pharaoh, the Ad, and Thamud became examples: "We made them a people of the past, and We made an example of them to later ages." (43:56)

Allah's punishment comes only when He is immensely provoked and angered. His servants must avoid all the things He hates, and which He has declared forbidden.

"Truly every king has a sanctuary, and truly Allah's sanctuary is His prohibitions." (*Al-Bukhari, Muslim*). And Allah jealously guards His sanctuary; so beware of trespassing!

Disobedience to Allah carries its own punishment. Allah's Law must be preserved; otherwise, the one who violates it will be the first to suffer. "Those on whom My anger descends, are hurled to ruin." (20:81)

"We made them a people of the past, and We made an example of them to later ages."
(43:56)

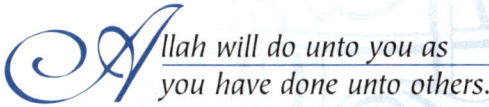

Allah will do unto you as you have done unto others.

AL-'AFUW

The Forgiving

"Allah is the All-pardoner, the Oft-forgiving." (22:60)

Allah pardons the sins of His servants. Out of gentleness and love He ignores their misdeeds or blots them out altogether, if they forsake evil and repent. "It is He who accepts repentance from His servants and pardons evil deeds." (42:25)

Perfect pardon comes from the Strong One who, though throughly capable of retribution, prefers clemency and forgiveness. "He can cause them to perish for their misdeeds; there are many sins that He pardons" (42:34). Allah pardons His servants for their mistakes, their forgetfulness, and for what they have done under duress.

He also pardons us for our evil intentions unless they materialize into evil deeds; if they do not, and we reject those intentions altogether, He records this as a fully good deed.

To be pardoned is the wish of every servant. The Prophet, peace be upon him, recommended that, on the Night of Power, one should say, "*Allahumma*! You are the All-pardoner, You love pardoning, so pardon me" (*Tirmidhi*); and he said, "Ask Allah for pardon and well-being in this life and the Hereafter." (*Tirmidhi*)

"He can cause them to perish for their misdeeds; there are many sins that He pardons."
(42:34)

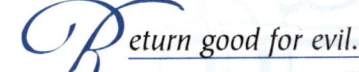

Return good for evil.

AL-RA'UF — The Gentle

"Surely Allah is Most kind, All-compassionate." (24:20)

Allah is the Most Kind. His kindness is ultimate mercy. It means granting forgiveness to the sinner, and the upholding of integrity for the obedient. "Allah would never let your faith become fruitless—truly, Allah is Most Kind with people, and All-compassionate." (2:143)

Allah's injunctions are for the good and benefit of mankind. They are never harsh. "Allah wishes to lighten your burdens, for man was created a weakling." (4:28)

Any temporary swerving from duty due to the weakness of human nature in the face of difficulties or temptations will be readily forgiven, if one repents. This happened to some of the Companions of the Prophet, peace be upon him: "When some of them were on the point of losing heart, He turned towards them;

surely He was Most Kind to them, and All-compassionate." (9:117)

Allah puts kindness in the hearts of whoever He will. "We put in the hearts of those who followed him tenderness and mercy." (57:27)

"Allah wishes to lighten your burdens, for man was created a weakling."
(4:28)

You have two qualities which Allah and His messenger love,— fortitude and gentleness.

The Lord of the Kingdom

MALIKU'L-MULK — مَالِكُ الْمُلْكِ

"O Allah, Sovereign of all sovereignty." (3:26)

Allah is the Lord of the Kingdom, in His hand is all that is good. "You bestow sovereignty on whom You will and take it away from whom You please." (3:26)

Allah is the sole Owner of all creation. "Do you not know that to Allah belongs the kingdom of the heavens and the earth?" (2:107)

Everything in this world is subjected to Allah's will and law, whether this is to the liking of human beings or not. "To Allah bow all who are in the heavens and on the earth, willingly or unwillingly." (13:15)

But the happy ones indeed are those who acknowledge His supremacy and His Overlordship and follow His path willingly and with love. "Whoever submits his will to Allah, being a doer of good works, shall be rewarded by his Lord, and they shall have nothing to fear or repent." (2:112)

On Resurrection Day, Allah holds the earth and folds the sky in His Right Hand and then says, "I am the King; where are the kings of the earth?" (*Muslim*)

"To Allah bow all who are in the heavens and on the earth, willingly or unwillingly."
(13:15)

Meet your Lord with a clean record.

The Lord of Majesty and Generosity

ذوالجلال والأكرام
DHU'L-JALAL WA'L-IKRAM

"Blessed be the Name of Your Lord, Possessor of Majesty and Nobility." (55:78)

Allah is the Possessor of Majesty: loftiness with supreme honour. It sums up all the noble qualities which we associate with the Beautiful Names of Allah.

Ikram (Nobility) comprises (1) extreme generosity (hence, *Al-Karim*) and (2) honour. Allah deserves to be honoured by the beings He has created. "O you who believe! Bow down and prostrate yourselves and serve your Lord, and do good." (22:77)

Allah has also conferred honour on man. "We have honoured the Children of Adam" (17:70). He raised man to a position above brute creation by giving him his spiritual faculties and powers of reasoning.

This is a name to call when praising and glorifying the

Lord. "O Allah: You are the All-peaceable and from You comes peace, blessed may You be, Possessor of Majesty and Nobility." (*Muslim*)

God has imposed certain moral obligations, do not abrogate them; He has forbidden certain things, do not indulge in them; He has laid down certain limits, do not transgress them; He is silent on certain matters, do not knowingly argue over them. (*Ad-Darqutni*)

"O you who believe! Bow down and prostrate yourselves and serve your Lord, and do good."
(22:77)

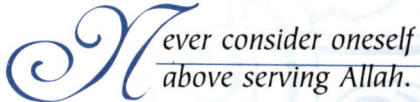

Never consider oneself above serving Allah.

The Just
AL-MUQSIT

"Say: 'My Lord has commanded fairness.'" (7:29)

Perfect fairness is an attribute of Allah—an attribute so momentous, and often impatiently questioned, that Allah Himself bears witness to it: "Allah bears witness—and the angels, and men possessed of knowledge—that there is no god but He, upholding justice." (3:18)

He recognizes any good, however little, which He finds in people, and rewards them beyond all measure. Why would Allah chastise you if you are thankful, and believe in Him?" (4:147)

So, good deeds, even those of the unbelievers, do not go unheeded; however, there is a difference: The Prophet, peace be upon him, said, "If the unbeliever does a good deed, he is recompensed in this world; as for the believer, Allah saves His divine requital for him in the Hereafter, but rewards him with earthly provision in this world for his obedience." (*Muslim*)

To stand out firmly for justice is to be a witness for Allah, even if it is against our own interests, or the interests of those who are dear to us. "O believers, conduct yourselves with justice, and bear true witness before Allah, even though it be against yourselves, or your parents and kinsmen. Whether the man be rich or poor; Allah knows better about them both. Then do not be led by caprice, lest you swerve from the truth; for if you distort your testimony or decline to give it, know that Allah is aware of all the things you do." (4:135)

"Allah bears witness—and the angels, and men possessed of knowledge—that there is no god but He, upholding justice"
(3:18)

To collaborate in injustice is sinful.

The Gatherer

AL-JAMI'

"Our Lord, it is You who will gather all mankind before You on a day which will indisputably come." (3:9)

Allah has the power to gather the bones and particles of every body, from wherever they may be scattered, for the Reckoning. "What, does man think We shall not gather his bones? Indeed, We are able to remould his very fingertips." (75:3-4)

Allah will gather all mankind, from the beginning of their race, and crowd them together. It will be a dreadful scene, and the deeds of the wrongdoers will be declared for all to witness. "Such is the Day of Decision. We will assemble you all with past generations." (77:38)

In the Hereafter, Allah gathers the good in Paradise, where they may enjoy each other's company. "We shall unite the true believers and those of their offspring who followed them in belief" (52:21). And the good man's prayer is: "Allow me to die in true submission, and join me with the righteous." (12:101)

The bad, on the other hand, are thrown together in Hell, cursing each other. "Allah will gather all the hypocrites and the unbelievers in Hell." (4:140)

He also unites the hearts of the pious in love and compassion. "If you had expended all that is in the earth, you could not have brought their hearts together; but Allah brought their hearts together." (8:63)

"Such is the Day of Decision. We will assemble you all with past generations." (77:38)

He whose heart is free from hatred will enter Heaven.

The Self-sufficient

"Indeed, Allah does not need you, but you need Him." (47:38)

Allah is free of need, He is independent of all His creation. He owns everything and everybody; while people own nothing except what He allows them to have; and they depend on Him for their livelihood. "To Allah belongs all that is in the heavens and on the earth; surely Allah is Self-sufficient, and worthy of praise." (31:26)

Most of all, Allah does not need a companion. "They say, 'Allah has taken to Him a son'. Glory be to Him! He is Self-sufficient." (10:68)

Allah does not benefit from our servitude, nor does He lose by people's disbelief. "O My servants! Were the first and the last of you, the human and the jinn of you, to be as pious as the most pious heart of any of you, that would not increase My kingdom in anything. O My servants! Were the first and the last of you, the human and the jinn of you, to be as wicked as the most wicked heart of any of you, that would not decrease My kingdom in anything." (*Muslim*)

Whatever good we do will be returned to us. "Whoever struggles for Allah's cause, struggles for his own gain; surely Allah is Self-sufficient, and needs no man's help." (29:6)

Moreover, man has the honour of lending to Allah. One may give to the poor and needy, but with the right intention in his mind, he may be dealing with Allah "Who is he that will lend Allah a good loan, and He will multiply it for him many times over?" (2:245)

"They say, 'Allah has taken to Him a son'. Glory be to Him! He is Self-sufficient."
(10:68)

Allah has all the answers we need.

AL-MUGHNI

"And it is He who gives wealth and riches." (53:48)

Allah is the Enricher who gives us material possessions and frees us from want. "Did He not find you needy, and enrich you?" (93:8)

Need should not cause us to disobey Him, thinking that wealth can be given by other beings. "If you fear poverty, Allah will surely enrich you from His bounty, if He will." (9:28)

Greater than the gift of material things is the blessing of satisfaction. "Richness is not abundance in material things, but the satisfaction of the soul" (*Al-Bukhari, Muslim*)

So, with faith, man is satisfied with very few worldly possessions, and aspires for no more. His happiness is derived from higher spiritual matters: the love of Allah and the hopes of entering His Paradise. "O my people! Surely this present life is but a passing enjoyment;

surely the world to come is an everlasting abode." (40:39)

To Him we turn in time of need. "*Allahumma*! Bestow upon me Your lawful [provision]; and enrich me with Your bounty as opposed to that of anyone else." (*Tirmidhi*)

"Did He not find you needy, and enrich you?"
(93:8)

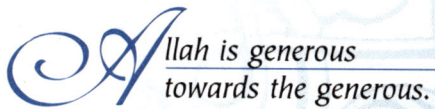

Allah is generous towards the generous.

AL-MANI'

The Withholder

"None can give what You withhold." (*Al-Bukhari, Muslim*)

Allah withholds His bounty from people, either because they do not deserve it, or to test them. If He wishes to deprive somebody of His bounty, is there any power that can interfere? "Who shall provide for you if He withholds His sustenance?" (67:21). If only people could appreciate the good things in life that they enjoy unawares. Let them imagine for a brief moment that one of the things they take for granted has disappeared or been rendered useless: "Have you considered the water you drink? Did you send it down from the clouds, or did We? If We pleased, We would make it salty; so why are you not thankful?" (56:68-70)

Allah withholds His Light from those who deliberately and obstinately reject the faith; who refuse His guidance and ignore all admonitions. So, He withdraws His grace and mercy from them. "We have put before them a barrier and behind them a barrier; and We have covered them, so that they cannot see." (36:9)

Al-Mani is also the One who defends His good servants against the powers of evil. "Assuredly, Allah will defend those who believe." (22:38)

"Who shall provide for you if He withholds His sustenance?"
(67:21)

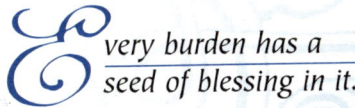

Every burden has a seed of blessing in it.

AL-DARR

"And if Allah afflicts you with evil, none can remove it but He." (6:17)

No affliction besets us or is removed from us except by Allah's permission. So, we must fear only Him, for fear of harm has always driven people of all civilizations to worshipping false gods. "Say: 'Shall we call on idols which can neither profit nor hurt us?'" (6:71)

Many occurrences, seemingly bad or arbitrary, are in reality works of wisdom, devised by the Omniscient One. Acceptance of this view of things is essential for our mental and spiritual well-being. Man is asked: "How can you bear patiently with that which is beyond your knowledge?" (18:68). Trust in Allah and in His higher wisdom, makes it possible for us to accept the inexplicable suffering around us.

If Allah chooses to afflict a man with misfortune, the faithful servant takes it as a blessing in disguise. "Any Muslim harmed by a thorn, or aught above it will be forgiven his bad deeds, and his sins will be shed like the leaves from a tree." (*Al-Bukhari, Muslim*)

Allah explains. "We afflicted them with misery and hardship so that they might be humble" (6:42). It is the spiritual experience that makes human beings better people. A misfortune is also a test of faith. "Do men think they will be left to say 'We believe,' and will not be tried?" (29:2). This Name should not be invoked by itself but in combination with "the Beneficent."

"How can you bear patiently with that which is beyond your knowledge?"
(18:68)

It is for Allah to judge man.

AL-NAFI'

The Beneficent

"Who created me, and Himself guides me, and Himself gives me food and drink, and, whenever I am sick, heals me." (26:78-80)

Man cannot earn any good for himself, nor remove any harm from himself except by the will of Allah. "Say: 'I have no power to acquire benefits for myself, or to avert evil from myself except as Allah will.'" (7:188)

Man's self-confidence should not blind him. One does his best, knowing that real good comes from Allah. "Do not pray to idols which can neither help nor harm you" (10:106). Very often, men seek beneficence of the wrong beings, though false gods have always, been, directly or indirectly, a source of oppression and evil. "He calls upon one who is likelier to hurt him, than help him: an evil protector indeed, and an evil friend." (22:13)

Thus, Allah is the Beneficent One who, alone, is worthy of the name. "Know that if the Nations were to gather together to benefit you with anything, it would benefit you only with something that Allah had already prescribed for you." (*Tirmidhi*)

"Say: 'I have no power to acquire benefits for myself, or to avert evil from myself except as Allah will.'"
(7:188)

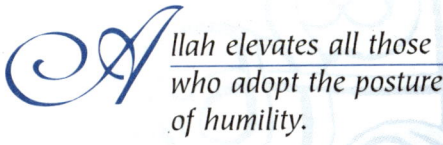

Allah elevates all those who adopt the posture of humility.

The Light

AL-NUR

"Allah is the Light of the heavens and the earth." (24:35)

Allah is the Ultimate, Manifest Light, Light in and by Himself, not kindled from other lights. Physical light is in no sense similar to His. His Light in this world is His true religion: the Oneness of Allah, His Law, and knowledge of Him established in the believers' hearts. "Believe in Allah and His Messenger, and in the Light We have sent down." (64:8)

This Light He will perfect, i.e., make it penetrate the hearts of men and shine all the brighter in their eyes, in spite of the enmity of the evil ones. "They desire to extinguish with their mouths the light of Allah, but Allah will perfect His Light, though the unbelievers be averse." (71:8)

Anyone who turns his back to the true Light is in complete darkness mentally, spiritually and morally." Not equal are the blind and the seeing man, nor are the darkness and the light." (35:20)

So, a believer's prayer is to be enveloped in such light: "*Allahumman*: Put light in my heart, light in my tongue, light in my sight, light in my hearing, light on my right, light on my left, light from above me, light from beneath me, light in front of me and light from behind me. Put light in my soul, and give me great light." (*Al-Bukhari, Muslim*)

"Believe in Allah and His Messenger, and in the Light We have sent down."
(64:8)

The preacher of Allah's word wishes people well, no matter how they treat him.

AL-HADI

The Guide

"Your Lord suffices as a guide and as a helper." (25:31)

Allah guides hearts to the truth, and to what is good for people spiritually and materially: "And assuredly Allah will guide those who believe to a straight path." (22:54)

The more sincere and the purer our faith is, the more Allah guides us to understand His ways and accept His judgment. "As for those who follow the right path, He will increase their guidance and show them the way to righteousness" (47:17). "Surely those who believe, and do deeds of righteousness, their Lord will guide them through their belief." (10:9)

Allah's guidance comes to those who search for it: "Those who struggle for Our cause We shall surely guide them to Our way" (29:69). Allah guides all creatures, even the unintelligent ones, to act as best suits their interests. Instinct is guidance given by Allah. Even the cell "knows" right course. "Our Lord is He who gave everything its distinctive form, then rightly guided it" (20:50). "And We guided him to the right path whether he was thankful or unthankful." (76:3)

In times of perplexity, one should turn to Allah for guidance and call Him by this Name. "O My servants, all of you are astray, except for those I have guided, so seek guidance of Me and I shall guide you." (*Muslim*)

"Our Lord, let not our hearts go astray after You have guided us." (3:8)

"Surely those who believe, and do deeds of righteousness, their Lord will guide them through their belief."
(10:9)

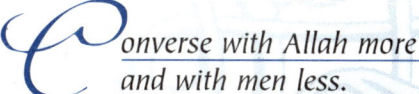

Converse with Allah more and with men less.

AL-BADI'

The Innovative Creator

"The Innovative Creator of the heavens and the earth." (2:117)

Allah created the universe without any pre-existing mode. It is full of beauty, magnificence, and order. How can man, seeing all this, fail to see the Hand of Allah behind it? "Have they not beheld heaven above them, how We have built it, and decked it out beautifully, and it has no cracks? And the earth—We spread it out, and set upon it immoveable mountains, and We produced from it every kind of delectable plant." (50:6-7)

Everything we behold is uniquely designed and made for us to contemplate. These are signs in His Creation leading us to believe in the power and wisdom of the One God. "Do they not consider how the camel was created, how heaven was raised on high, how the mountains were set down, how the earth was levelled flat?" (88:17-20). Wonders upon wonders are disclosed in the constitution of every being.

Al-Badi also implies the Unique; no one is similar to Him in the Self, in Qualities and in Actions. "He is the Innovative Creator of the heavens and the earth; how should He have a son, seeing that He has no consort and He created all things?" (6:101)

>
>
> *"Do they not consider how the camel was created, how heaven was raised on high, how the mountains were set down, how the earth was levelled flat?"* (88:17-20)

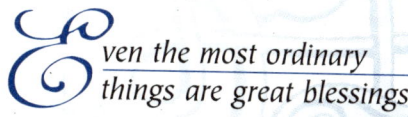

Even the most ordinary things are great blessings.

AL-BAQI

The Everlasting

"Allah is better and more abiding." (20:73)

Allah will never cease to exist. Any dependent being will terminate once his support is cut off; but Allah's existence does not depend on any factor or cause. "All things shall perish, except Himself." (28:88)

Man-made glory and splendour will pass away; the universe will come to an end at the appointed time; but He will live forever. "All that dwells upon the earth is doomed to die. But the Face of Your Lord, majestic and splendid, will abide forever" (55:27)

The wise man will prefer the pleasure of his Lord the Abiding, to the momentary gratification of this evanescent world. "Whatever you possess comes to an end, but Allah's reward is everlasting" (16:96). What is in Allah's power to give is "a garden as vast as the heavens and earth, prepared for the god-fearing" (3:133); a lasting pleasure.

On the Day of Judgement, no step shall man stir until he has answered questions on five aspects of his wordly existence: his life and how he spent it; his knowledge and what use he has made of it; his wealth, how he acquired it and how he has spent it; and his body and how he has utilized it. (*At-Tirmidhi*)

"All that dwells upon the earth is doomed to die. But the Face of Your Lord, majestic and splendid, will abide forever"
(55:27)

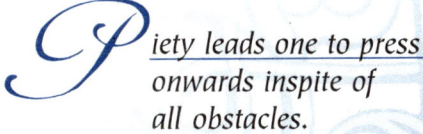

Piety leads one to press onwards inspite of all obstacles.

The Inheritor

AL-WARITH

"We Ourselves are the Inheritors." (28:58)

Allah is the Inheritor to whom shall revert all that survive the physical death of mankind. "Surely We shall inherit the earth and all that are upon it, and unto Us they shall be returned." (19:40)

Al-Warith is also the One who bequeaths the heritage of the earth to whoever He will. "Surely the earth is Allah's and He bequeaths it to whom He will among His servants. Happy shall be the lot of the righteous." (7:128)

So, His promise is: "The earth shall be the inheritance of My righteous servants" (21:105). He brings low the arrogant and insolent nation, and gives its heritage to another, maybe less strong, but righteous. "It was our will to favour those who were oppressed in the land, and to make them leaders, among men, and to bestow on them a noble inheritance, and to give them power in the land." (28:5-6)

The most precious thing Allah bequeaths to people is Paradise, "which We shall give as an inheritance to those of Our servants who are god-fearing." (19:63)

"Surely the earth is Allah's and He bequeaths it to whom He will among His servants. Happy shall be the lot of the righteous."
(7:128)

Walk in Allah's way instead of asking Him to do things your way.

The Guide
AL-RASHID

"And furnish us with rectitude in our affair." (18:10)

Allah is perfect in rectitude, great in wisdom. His designs are always right.

He is the One who guides to rectitude. He has shown us the Righ Path in the teachings of His Prophets, so clearly that human nature will readily follow it. There shall be no compulsion in religion. True guidance has now become distinct from error." (2:256)

The perfect essence of His guidance is in the Holy Qur'an. "We have heard a wondrous Qur'an, guiding to rectitude." (72:2)

There is only One Righ Path, but there are many wrong paths. Once the individual abandons the Right Path, he is left to his own limited means, and will be virtually lost. "Whoever Allah guides is rightly guided, but whoever He leads astray, shall not find a protector to direct him." (18:17)

We should pray, as the Prophet, peace be upon him, did: "*Allahumma!* Inspire me with rectitude, and keep me from the evil of myself." (*At-Tirmidhi*)

"We have heard a wondrous Qur'an, guiding to rectitude."
(72:2)

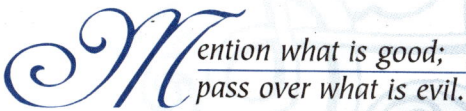

Mention what is good; pass over what is evil.

AL-SABUR

The Forbearing

"Bear with the unbelievers, and let them be awhile:" (86:17)

Allah is Patient with the unbelievers and the disobedient. They may ride high, free and arrogant; but they are not safe and secure forever; forbearance does not mean approval of evil. Allah does not punish them right away, but allows them time so that they may turn to Him. "Allah may give some respite to the evil-doer; but once He takes him He does not release him." (Al-Bukhari, Muslim)

Restraining one's anger in the face of a grave wrong needs both patience and strength, Allah is Long-suffering, for He is the Almighty. "Nobody is more patient in the face of injurious words than Allah: They attribute to Him a son, while He provides for them and gives them health." (Al-Bukhari)

Allah orders Muslims to be patient when His Fate strikes;

where they have no means to remove the evil; and when confronted by temptations. "Allah loves the patient" (3:146). He supports them. "Be patient then; Allah will grant you patience" (16:127). And He changes their pain and misery into faith, strength and honour. "We appointed from among them leaders giving guidance at Our command, when they endured patiently, and had firm faith in Our signs." (32:24)

"Nobody is more patient in the face of injurious words than Allah: They attribute to Him a son, while He provides for them and gives them health."
(Al-Bukhari)

No affliction is worse than hardness of the heart.

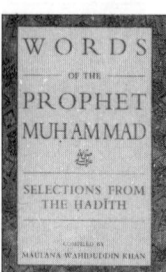
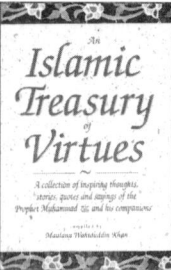

Printed in India